What Gregg Allison and Chris Castaldo have done in this important book is unique: they carefully explore the many areas where Protestants and Catholics agree but also disagree. I've seen exhortations to unity, and I've seen polemics for division, but I've never seen one volume deal so well with both commonality and also disagreement. Knowing their personal ministry, though, I'm not surprised that Allison and Castaldo exhibit such grace alongside truth.

Collin Hansen, editorial director, the Gospel Coalition, and author, *Blind Spots: Becoming a Courageous, Compassionate, and Commissioned Church*

This book is a model of gracious and principled dialogue, as much for its tone as its content. I heartily recommended it for all who care about theology and the particular conversation between evangelical Protestants and Roman Catholics.

Gerald Hiestand, Executive Director, the Center for Pastor Theologians

This book blows a welcome breeze into the stifling and oppressive debates between Protestants and Catholics. Too often each side labels the other a "false church" and refuses to see the good the other tradition offers. Allison and Castaldo refuse to be this simplistic—not to mention uncharitable—in their approach. Congenial in their tolerance while never obscuring real differences, the authors lay out the main points of disagreement between these two Christian traditions. If you are a Protestant with a Catholic in your life, or vice versa, you need this book in your library.

Bryan Litfin, Professor of Theology, Moody Bible Institute

The Unfinished Reformation is an accessible, well-written explanation of Catholic beliefs, Protestant beliefs, and how the two relate. The layperson can read this book and feel equipped to have well-rounded conversations about faith with his

Ed Stetzer, Billy Graham D

T0053466

Many Christians are aware that there are fundamental differences between Protestants and Roman Catholics but are unsure exactly what these differences are or how much they really matter. Some may regard them as trivial, while others may struggle to see how there can be Christians in both groups. *The Unfinished Reformation* sets out clearly and simply where the differences lie. The differences are not minimized, nor are they magnified. Where Protestants have often misrepresented Roman Catholics—this is pointed out. At the same time there is no pretense that no differences exist. This book is to be warmly commended to those wishing to understand these issues better.

Tony Lane, Professor of Historical Theology,
London School of Theology

This is the best treatment I have read on understanding what continues to unite and divide Catholics and Protestants. While considering the historic roots of the Reformation in the sixteenth century, Gregg Allison and Chris Castaldo also remain sensitive to the significant doctrinal shifts of the twentieth century and our contemporary context. They are informed but not pedantic, accessible but not simplistic. Both scholar and layperson will benefit. I heartily recommend this book to Catholics and Protestants alike who desire an honest and thoughtful way to approach the other side of the "divided family."

Rev. Dr. Camden M. Bucey, President, Reformed Forum; Pastor,
Hope Orthodox Presbyterian Church, Grayslake, Illinois

Allison and Castaldo have provided a book that is both timely and thoughtful—a book that at the same time looks fondly on the Reformation yet asks the important question of these reforms for today. Their approach is especially sensitive to the realities of divided families, one Catholic and one Protestant, yet aware of how Catholics and Protestants find themselves united on struggles to end abortion. This is a book that will educate the novice and provoke thought in the expert.

Ryan M. Reeves, Associate Professor of Historical Theology and Dean
of Jacksonville Campus of Gordon-Conwell Theological Seminary

THE UNFINISHED REFORMATION

GREGG R. ALLISON

The Baker Compact Dictionary of Theological Terms

Roman Catholic Theology and Practice: An Evangelical Assessment

Sojourners and Strangers: The Doctrine of the Church

Historical Theology: An Introduction to Christian Doctrine

CHRIS CASTALDO

*The Grammar of Justification: The Doctrines of Peter Martyr Vermigli
and John Henry Newman and Their Ecumenical Implications*

Talking with Catholics about the Gospel: A Guide for Evangelicals

*Una Fe Renovada: Historia, doctrina, experiencia
y el peregrinar del católico y el evangélico*

Holy Ground: Walking with Jesus as a Former Catholic

THE UNFINISHED REFORMATION

WHAT UNITES AND DIVIDES CATHOLICS AND PROTESTANTS AFTER 500 YEARS

GREGG ALLISON
AND CHRIS CASTALDO

ZONDERVAN

The Unfinished Reformation
Copyright © 2016 by Gregg Allison and Chris Castaldo

This title is also available as a Zondervan ebook.

This title is also available as a Zondervan audio book.

Requests for information should be addressed to:
Zondervan, *3900 Sparks Dr. SE, Grand Rapids, Michigan 49546*

Library of Congress Cataloging-in-Publication Data

Names: Allison, Gregg R., author.
Title: The unfinished Reformation : why Catholics and Protestants are still divided 500 years later / Gregg Allison and Chris Castaldo.
Description: Grand Rapids : Zondervan, 2016.
Identifiers: LCCN 2016019024 | ISBN 9780310527930 (softcover)
Subjects: LCSH: Protestant churches--Relations--Catholic Church. | Catholic Church--Relations--Protestant churches.
Classification: LCC BX4818.3 .A45 2016 | DDC 280/.042--dc23 LC record available at https://lccn.loc.gov/2016019024

The authors wish to thank Baker Book House for their permission to quote from Gregg R. Allison's *Baker Compact Dictionary of Theological Terms* (Grand Rapids: Baker, 2016).

Cover design: John Hamilton
Interior design: Kait Lamphere

Printed in the United States of America

HB 05.06.2022

We dedicate this book to our siblings:

Terry Allison,
who as a husband, father, grandfather,
and pastor to hundreds and hundreds of children,
is a stellar example of faithfulness, perseverance,
and fruitfulness in ministry.

Jeanette Castaldo,
your vibrant witness for Christ—
your kindness, strength, generosity, and love—
bears testimony to the beauty of the gospel.
We rise up and call you blessed.

The dove descending breaks the air
With flame of incandescent terror
Of which the tongues declare
The one discharge from sin and error.
The only hope, or else despair
Lies in the choice of pyre or pyre—
To be redeemed from fire by fire.

T. S. Eliot, *Four Quartets*

Contents

Contents

Abbreviations

ANF   *Ante-Nicene Fathers*, eds. Alexander Roberts, James
Donaldson, Philip Schaff, and Henry Wace, 10 vols.
(Peabody, Mass.: Hendrickson, 1994).

CCC   *Catechism of the Catholic Church* (New York: Doubleday,
1995). The number(s) following this abbreviation refer to
the section(s), not the page number(s), of the *Catechism*;
e.g., CCC 1459–1460.

Institutes   John Calvin, *Institutes of the Christian Religion*, ed. John
T. McNeill, trans. Ford Lewis Battles (Philadelphia:
Westminster, 1960).

JD   The Lutheran World Federation and the Catholic
Church, *Joint Declaration on the Doctrine of Justification*.
Available at: http://www.vatican.va/roman_curia/
pontifical_councils/chrstuni/documents/rc_pc
_chrstuni_doc_31101999_cath-luth-joint-declaration
_en.html

LW   Martin Luther, *Luther's Works*, eds. Jaroslav Pelikan,
          Hilton C. Oswald, and Helmut T. Lehmann, 55 vols.
          (St. Louis: Concordia, 1955–1986).

NPNF1   *Nicene and Post-Nicene Fathers*, eds. Alexander Roberts,
          James Donaldson, Philip Schaff, and Henry Wace, 1st
          series, 14 vols. (Peabody, Mass.: Hendrickson, 1994).

NPNF2   *Nicene and Post-Nicene Fathers*, eds. Alexander Roberts,
          James Donaldson, Philip Schaff, and Henry Wace, 2nd
          series, 14 vols. (Peabody, Mass.: Hendrickson, 1994).

Schaff   Philip Schaff, *Creeds of Christendom*, 3 vols. (New York:
          Harper, 1877–1905).

Acknowledgments

This book started with a search for clarity.

A student of Tony Lane's had asked him to recommend a resource that surveys the commonalities and differences between Roman Catholic and evangelical Protestant theology with reference to the Reformation. Tony inquired with Chris Castaldo, soliciting his opinion, who in turn asked a few friends at the Catholic/Protestant intersection: Leonardo De Chirico in Rome, Mark Gilbert in Australia, Ralph MacKenzie in San Diego, and Gregg Allison in Louisville. Gregg was the first to respond: "I can't think of one, Chris; we should coauthor such a book."

When the other leaders also identified the lack of such a book, Chris realized that Gregg was onto something. Gregg then proposed the idea to Ryan Pazdur at Zondervan, and shortly thereafter, Ryan and Chris discussed the concept over coffee. It was somewhere in the middle of those cappuccinos that plans for the book stepped into the realm of reality.

In addition to thanking Ryan and the staff at Zondervan, we wish to also recognize colleagues and friends whose input has contributed to this project. First, we would like to thank our friend, Leonardo De Chirico. Leo's articulation of the Christ-Church interconnection has been enormously helpful in explaining the ecclesiological self-understanding of Catholicism. Similarly, we would also like to thank Henri Blocher, who has specifically applied this paradigm to the sacraments. We are indebted to Tony Lane for his work on the doctrine of justification, particularly in Regensburg, Trent, Calvin, and contemporary Catholicism. And we are grateful for numerous Catholic friends and colleagues, particularly Mike Brummond, Eduardo Echeverria, Fr. Dermot Fenlon, and Brett Salkeld.

If readers would like to go deeper into the topics addressed in this book, Gregg has written *Roman Catholic Theology and Practice: An Evangelical Assessment*, and Chris has written *Holy Ground: Walking with Jesus as a Former Catholic* and *Talking with Catholics about the Gospel*.

We would like to thank Sojourn Community Church, where Gregg serves as an elder, and New Covenant Church in Naperville, where Chris serves as lead pastor. You are the readership that we had in mind throughout the writing of this volume. Finally, we wish to thank our spouses, Nora and Angela, and our families, whose love and support has made this work possible.

Introduction:
What Happened 500 Years Ago?

Go to a prayer vigil outside an abortion clinic and you will find Protestants and Roman Catholics standing together in solidarity. Probe the ranks of marriage's defenders and you will find the two groups united. Or step into a concert of prayer in which Dutch Reformed and Hispanic Catholic congregations are petitioning God in unison. You may be drawn to ask an important question: Is the Reformation finished?

We cannot judge whether it is finished, of course, unless we understand how it began. Looking back five hundred years confronts us with an era of momentous change in which many Christians desired renewed faith. Men and women returned to Scripture and the writings of the early church, igniting what some have described as "another Pentecost" or "light after darkness." Five centuries later, we call it the Reformation.

Not everyone, however, regarded the movement as divine illumination. Some viewed the quest for renewal as a menacing threat, opening the way to doctrinal error, political turmoil, and social disorder. At the center of this disagreement was the question: To whom did God give authority to define Christian faith? Did it belong to the institution of the Roman Catholic Church? Or was Scripture its own interpreter?

The Reformation emerged in the tailwind of several broad developments in European society, including urbanization, increased affluence, and a rise in literacy. Meanwhile, a growing sense of anticlericalism became a focus of discontent with the Church. More significantly, however, the Reformation was brought to life by theology. In addition to the fundamental debate over religious authority, questions about salvation and calling in the world were being answered in fresh ways. Many became convinced that ordinary Christians (individuals without priestly ordination or academic degrees) could read and understand the Bible without the teaching office of the Roman Church. In reading the text, Christians recognized divine acceptance, or justification, as coming to sinners by faith alone. And they perceived that the Christian priesthood extended to every believer, endowing such temporal vocations as farming and smithery with new dignity and purpose.

Martin Luther is commonly identified as the pioneer of the Reformation. We recognize, of course, that there were forerunners—men such as John Wycliffe and Jan Hus[1]—but from Luther the opening salvo would come. The nailing of his Ninety-Five Theses (1517) and his famous "stand" at the Diet of Worms (1521) symbolize the daring spirit of the movement.[2] What began as opposition to the sale of indulgences (a remission of temporal punishment by paying money to the church) became an exposé of church corruption, even to the point of challenging the pope's authority. It was around the same time that Huldrych Zwingli started preaching reform in Zurich, followed by Martin Bucer's work in Strasbourg. In a few short years, the disciples of this first generation of Reformers would emerge from the shadows, leaders such as Philip Melanchthon, Heinrich Bullinger, John Calvin, Peter Martyr Vermigli, and Thomas Cranmer.[3] To these men would fall the task of defining the movement in precise terms. A copious amount of biblical commentaries, theological treatises, confessions of faith, catechisms, sermons, and much more bear eloquent testimony to their productivity.

A Map of Early Sixteenth-Century Europe

Evangelicals (subsequently called "Protestants"), however, did not have a monopoly on church reform. For example, it was at Easter of 1511 when Gasparo Contarini (later made Cardinal) experienced an evangelical renewal similar to Luther. Contarini came to recognize that sinners are justified by the righteousness of Christ, appropriated by faith, apart from meritorious works. In due time, a movement grew to include other Roman Catholic notables: Juan de Valdés, Cardinal Giacomo Sadoleto, Cardinal Giovanni Morone, Cardinal Reginald Pole, and Cardinal Tommaso Badia.[4] However, the evangelical impulse of Catholic renewal was short lived. In 1545, the Council of Trent convened to oppose the growing movement and cut a new path. As one Catholic historian has described it:

> [The Council of Trent's] spirituality was then sacramental, centered on the Eucharist. It was exacting, making stiff demands on its practitioners: self-discipline, self-control, and regularity in prayer. It was practical in the way it closely associated good works with self-improvement. And finally, in accordance with the dominant cultural trend of the times, it was humanistic—at least in its assumption that each person had it in his power, to some degree, to determine his own fate.[5]

DEFINING THE REFORMATION

So what was the sixteenth-century Reformation? The answer may be more elusive than we realize. Should we supply the article, "*the* Reformation," or is it better to speak of multiple reformations? What were its primary causes and central aims? When did it begin, and when did it end, if indeed it has?

To understand the sixteenth-century Reformation, we must begin by defining the term. The medievals used the word *reformatio* to describe the enterprise of repairing an inadequate state of affairs by returning to an earlier expression of faith. This idea, for example, is what Pope Innocent III had in mind when he convened the Fourth Lateran Council (1213; begun in 1215) "for the reformation of the universal church." This movement, and others like it, sought to manifest deeper dimensions of God's truth through ethical and spiritual renewal.

In the opening years of the sixteenth century, the faithful expressed criticism of ecclesiastical institutions and offered proposals for renewal. The Fifth Lateran Council (1512–1517), supposedly a "reform" council, was therefore teeming with reformation potential. During the Council, Cardinal Giles of Viterbo (Italy; 1469–1532) spoke for many who desired a greater measure of personal faith when he declared: "Men must be changed by religion, not religion by men."[6] Such religious hunger sent thoughtful Christians to reexamine the roots of their faith. This examination produced a wide range of proposals aimed at bringing reformation, the form of which differed depending upon region and time period.

In subsequent years, the tepid state of the church persisted. This was due to several factors, such as:

- an appalling standard of morality by Renaissance popes such as Alexander VI (reigned 1492–1503) and his family whom he gifted with privilege and wealth;
- the ongoing tension between the Catholic emperor, Charles V, and his popes, which embroiled church leadership in political affairs of the Papal States;
- the rise of democratic values by public intellectuals such as Erasmus, which called into question elements of Catholic tradition;
- the construction of Saint Peter's Basilica in Rome, which encouraged the selling of religious benefits such as indulgences;
- and an inadequate education of priests, whose ministries were often marked by veniality and superstition.

Thus, the need for renewal was becoming increasingly apparent.

Historians often look to the year 1517, when Luther nailed his Ninety-Five Theses to the church door at Wittenberg, as the starting point to the Protestant Reformation. We remember, however, that Luther did not intend to leave the Catholic Church in 1517. A cursory reading of the Theses reveals his deference to the pope. Evidently, Luther believed that if the pontiff were only made aware of the abuses occurring in Germany, he would bring reform. As Luther wrote in Thesis 50, "If a pope knew how much people were being charged for an indulgence—he would prefer to demolish St. Peter's." But in the year 1521, Luther was expelled from the church.

In light of the above, we recognize "reformation of the sixteenth century" (without the article) to describe a widespread desire for, and movement toward, greater fidelity in the areas of theology, pastoral care, and overall piety. Here, the notion of an "always reforming church" (*ecclesia semper reformanda*) emerges as a driving force, a conviction that repudiates the status quo in the active pursuit of dynamic faith.[7] The idea of ongoing reform is fundamental to Protestant (and to some degree also Roman Catholic) Christianity.

More specifically, "*the* Reformation" describes an array of religious protests and initiatives of renewal that spread through Europe during the sixteenth century. To speak of the Reformation, therefore, is not to speak of a unified movement with a single leader; rather, it was a collection of disparate movements. For instance, one may speak of the "magisterial Reformation" (reform movements such as Lutheranism that were supported and enabled by magistrates, or political leaders), or the "radical" or "left wing" Reformation (non-institutionalized churches, such as Anabaptists, that broke away from the centuries-old state-church structure). One may also choose to distinguish Reformation movements by geographic region such as the Lutheran Reformation in Germany and Scandinavia, the Calvinist Reformation in Switzerland and the Netherlands, the Anglican Reformation in Great Britain, and the Radical Reformation in Germany, Switzerland, and the Netherlands. And there are some who would include Catholic renewal in this historical portrait, as in the Catholic Counter-Reformation. In short, there are numerous ways historians may slice the ecclesial onion to illustrate the profound difference between reform movements of the sixteenth century.

Granting the varied and complex shape of sixteenth-century reform, there is nevertheless a discernable core of convictions that defines the Reformation. With the primacy of Scripture as God's supreme authority and the early church as a model, Protestant Reformers jettisoned universal papal authority and, at varying degrees, spurned traditional beliefs and customs that had grown up in medieval Catholicism (e.g., monastic vows, pilgrimages, veneration of the saints, indulgences). On the basis of biblical authority, they sought to reestablish the essence and organization of the church (if not also wider society) to bring it in line with Scripture.

Following from this commitment to Scripture, movements of the Reformation generally reduced the number of sacraments from the traditional seven to only two: baptism and the Lord's Supper.[8] Communicating the Bible to laypeople was a priority. While opinions varied on style of worship (e.g., the role of images, aesthetics, and music), there was widespread agreement on the need for lay participation and services that employed the vernacular (common) language. Such reforms tended to get traction in urban centers before penetrating rural society.

Finally, in breaking with their medieval past, the Reformers also forged a specific understanding of the doctrine of justification. In opposition to the Roman Catholic Council of Trent, the

Reformers distinguished between justification and sanctification, declaring that the former was a legal declaration of innocence based on the imputed righteousness of Christ. This distinctly Protestant understanding of justification transformed the experience of salvation for sixteenth-century people and inspired them in their ongoing walk with God.

THE IMPORTANCE OF ASKING IF THE REFORMATION IS FINISHED

Despite the many gains of the Protestants in the sixteenth century, there are numerous reasons to ask whether the Reformation is now finished. A decade ago, Mark Noll and Carolyn Nystrom wrote an insightful book on the subject entitled *Is the Reformation Over?: An Evangelical Assessment of Contemporary Roman Catholicism*. We shall consider the strengths and liabilities of their thesis in our next chapter. In the remainder of this introduction, however, we will offer five particular reasons why the question of the Reformation's enduring significance is now more relevant than ever.

1. Conflict in Families and Churches

According to The Pew Forum on Religion and Public Life, over 15 million former Catholics in the United States now attend Protestant churches.[9] With a growing Hispanic population, this number promises to grow in coming years. These individuals represent numerous dinner tables over which Protestant and Catholic family members discuss their faith. Despite good intentions, these conversations often crash and burn amidst misunderstanding, stereotypes, and injurious polemics. Can Protestants and Catholics discuss the gospel in a fruitful way, or are the cultural and theological obstacles insurmountable?

Married couples in which one is a Catholic and the other a Protestant have even more basic problems. Which church will they attend? Will their children participate in the Protestant youth group or the Catholic Church's equivalent? What about the sacraments of Holy Communion or Confirmation? Is it advisable or acceptable for these parents to permit their children to observe religious ceremonies across the Catholic/Protestant divide, even ones with which they earnestly disagree? Does affirmation of this kind constitute loving support or negligent compromise? Dilemmas such as these ultimately come down to a stark issue: To what extent do Catholics and Protestants recognize one another as brothers and sisters in the same apostolic faith?

If a person's position on this issue can determine the course of a conversation or a marriage, how much more will it determine the relationship between church bodies? Some Protestant groups and churches operate according to the assumption that fidelity to the gospel requires them to be explicitly anti-Catholic. This mindset grows out of a simple syllogism: Since the Catholic Church denies justification by faith alone, it denies the biblical gospel, and, therefore, is essentially advocating a counterfeit religion. Protestants with this conviction often, therefore, malign the Roman Catholic Church with the same polemical language that is found in the writings of the sixteenth-century Reformers. Collaboration on social issues (e.g., sanctity of life, protecting children, caring for the elderly) is dismissed out of hand, for to collaborate would be to compromise the gospel. The way we assess and navigate these personal dilemmas, practical problems, and institutional questions are, whether we intend it or not, a statement on the status and relevance of the Reformation.

2. The Attraction of Pope Francis

The office of the papacy is an enigma to most evangelical Protestants. The spectacle of medieval regalia, coats of arms, and the popemobile provoke curiosity, skepticism, and bewilderment. Add to these symbols the pope's monarchial titles, infallibility, and a standing army, and the portrait gets even more perplexing. Why, then, are some evangelicals flocking to Pope Francis?

In his book *Pope Francis' Revolution of Tenderness and Love*, Cardinal Walter Kasper offers a clue to the answer. He contends that Francis is not a liberal (as some pundits would suggest) but rather a "radical" in the etymological sense of being rooted (*radix*) in the person of Jesus. Emerging from this root is a blossoming of Christian virtue that smells to many evangelicals like the aroma of Christ. Accordingly, Francis is regarded as a transparent, down-to-earth kind of servant who prefers washing the feet of prison inmates to the traditional pomp and circumstance of the Vatican. Such qualities resonate with evangelicals who generally see themselves as egalitarian, compassionate, and action-oriented.

In a similar vein, evangelicals flock to Pope Francis because they resonate with his approach to theology, which is more pietistic than doctrinal. For example, during my (Chris's) time of interaction with close friends of Francis, nearly all of them quoted a statement for which the pontiff is evidently famous: "Let us put theologians on an island to discuss among themselves and we'll just get on with things." Similar sentiments may be heard among many evangelicals today. Unfortunately, when piety comes at the expense of doctrine, Christian faith becomes impoverished and subject to distortion. Therefore, we must study the contemporary significance of not just the piety but also the doctrine of the Reformation.

3. The Problem of Nicodemism

When people living in Catholic nations during the sixteenth century (e.g., Italy, France, Spain) supported the Reformation, they often faced a life-and-death choice. Depending upon their response to Catholic authorities during the Inquisition (a Catholic Church tribunal aimed at combating Protestantism), they may have been tortured, executed, or forced to flee into exile.[10] "Nicodemism" was applied to yet another option, the decision to keep one's Reformation convictions contained quietly and safely in the privacy of one's own heart without public expression.

John Calvin is commonly recognized as the one who popularized the term, using "Nicodemism" to describe external conformity on the part of reformed-minded Christians living in Catholic territories. Faced with the threat of oppression at the hands of Catholic authorities, such individuals chose silence over persecution. The covert nature of this approach is responsible for its clever name, as one historian explains: "The name is suggested by the biblical character of Nicodemus, who came to visit Jesus by night, under the cover of darkness, thus suggesting a piety of simulation based on the fear of persecution."[11]

According to most Protestant Reformers, Nicodemism was an unacceptable option. It was regarded as infidelity to Christ and a compromise of one's integrity. For example, Peter Martyr Vermigli explained to his congregation in Lucca, Italy, the reason why he fled north of the Alps instead of becoming a Nicodemite: "[You] are hardly unaware of the tortures which tormented my conscience because of the way of life which I was following. I had to live with countless superstitions every day [such as pilgrimages and the veneration of relics, that is, the remains of a saint]; not only did I have to perform [these] superstitious rites, but also I had to demand harshly that others do many things which were contrary to what I was thinking and teaching."[12]

How can Nicodemism possibly have relevance today when religious inquisitions are a thing of the past? The "new Nicodemism" is found among Catholics who study the Bible for themselves and whose beliefs are in fact more Protestant than Catholic. Even though such people read Scripture apart from the Magisterium (the official teaching office of the Catholic Church), no longer believe in such doctrines as purgatory, and are increasingly bothered by the Catholic emphasis on Mary, they nevertheless remain in the Catholic fold.

Why is this so? There are all sorts of reasons, but it commonly comes down to a commitment to one's ethnic or cultural background, a Catholic family member, or relationship to a local parish. It is valuable for such people to consider how the Reformation speaks to their religious identity and whether these implications call for expression.

4. Conversion among Catholicism and Protestantism

Conversion from Protestantism to Catholicism has received attention over recent years, partly on account of autobiographies that describe the movement. For example, in 1993, a Presbyterian graduate of Gordon-Conwell, Scott Hahn, published *Rome Sweet Home: Our Journey to Catholicism*. In 1994, Professor Thomas Howard wrote his story, *Lead, Kindly Light: My Journey to Rome*. Two years later, David Currie wrote *Born Fundamentalist, Born Again Catholic*. In 2009, Frank Beckwith, after his election to the presidency of the Evangelical Theological Society, wrote *Return to Rome: Confessions of an Evangelical Catholic*. In 2011, radio host and columnist Michael Coren wrote *Why Catholics Are Right*. And in the same year Professor Christian Smith of Notre Dame wrote his story in a how-to book titled *How to Go from Being a Good Evangelical to a Committed Catholic in Ninety-Five Difficult Steps*. These narratives and others like them have garnered considerable attention.

In light of the above, we are regularly asked to comment on how the movement toward Rome compares in size with the number of converts who have left the Catholic Church for Protestantism. Without objective data, answers to this question have been anecdotal. Thankfully, a 2015 survey by the Pew Research Center brings the picture into somewhat sharper focus.[13] Here is our summary:

In contrast with the unaffiliated (people who don't identify with any church or religion), Catholicism has experienced the greatest net losses due to religious migration. Nearly a third of all U.S. adults (31.7%) were raised Catholic, and most of them continue to identify as Catholics today. *But nearly 13% of all Americans are former Catholics*—people who no longer identify with the faith despite having been raised in the Catholic Church. By comparison, there are *far fewer converts to Catholicism; 2% of all U.S. adults* now identify as Catholics after having been raised in another religion or without a religion. This means that there are more than six former Catholics for every convert to Catholicism. No other religious group analyzed in the survey has experienced anything close to this ratio of losses to gains via religious switching.

According to this study, there are currently seven million converts to Catholicism, people who are now Catholic but who were raised in another religion (or in no religion at all). To be sure, that is a large number (exactly how many come from Protestantism, we don't know); however, while such individuals have entered the Catholic Church, there are also forty-one million who have left (13% of Americans). Among these disenchanted Catholics, sixteen million have found their way into Protestant churches of some sort.[14] Against this backdrop, we are left with the question of why individuals choose to cross the Catholic/Protestant divide, and, more germane to our subject, what these conversions say about the Reformation today.

5. Co-belligerence in American Society

These days, at least in the U.S., a palpable sense of urgency is found among conservative Christians. One might say that a new invasion of the Vandals is underway not unlike the fifth century when Augustine observed his beloved city under attack. In this case, however, it is not tribes of violent pirates in long boats who pose the threat. It is Hollywood and various forms of media peddling perversion in the name of entertainment, abortion merchants selling infant body parts, and social engineers redefining gender, marriage, and other biblically rooted institutions of Western civilization.

In response to the widespread displacement and exile of Christianity from mainstream culture, Catholics and Protestants are increasingly uniting in co-belligerence, what Timothy George describes as an "ecumenism of the trenches."[15] This movement of visible Christian unity is observed, for example, in Catholics and Protestants who pray together outside of abortion clinics, volunteer at food pantries, and associate with classical schools and in the marketplace. On Capitol Hill, Catholic and Protestant senators together draft bills for the common good. Ecumenism is promoted by publications such as *First Things*, *Pro Ecclesia*, and *Touchstone*; movements such as *Evangelicals and Catholics Together* and *Act 3* (a ministry that equips leaders for "missional ecumenism"); and documents such as the *Manhattan Declaration*. It is also observed in decisions of religious institutions such as the Presbyterian Church of America, which a decade ago revised its version of the Westminster Confession of Faith to exclude reference to the pope as antichrist. As the moral decline of culture increases, so does the need for unified churches that embody God's love and speak his truth together.

But where should the line be drawn? It is easy to recognize the need to embody the love of Christ in the public square. Also apparent is the need for this witness to come from a unified Christian body.

But to what extent can Catholics and Protestants stand together with doctrinal integrity? After all, Christians who are not in fellowship with the Catholic Church are still excluded from the Eucharist (the communion table). And many Protestants view the Catholic teaching on salvation as falling short of the biblical gospel. In view of these realities, to what extent is co-belligerence between Catholics and Protestants genuinely rooted in a common foundation of theological agreement? To what extent is the Reformation finished?

CONCLUSION: IS THE REFORMATION FINISHED?

The spread of the Reformation has spawned five centuries of extraordinary innovation and flexibility, but it has also generated a considerable amount of religious instability and even division. Perhaps the largest and deepest division is the one that runs along the Catholic and Protestant fault line. Suspicion, opposition, and religious strife have marked this relationship, with moments of outright conflict sporadically boiling over. Consider the fact that, just a few decades ago, Americans questioned the candidacy of presidential nominees on account of their membership in the Catholic Church.[16] At this moment of writing, however, five of the nine Supreme Court justices identify as Roman Catholic. It seems that things have changed.

But how much has changed? Greater familiarity and affinity with the pope, cooperation on social issues, the charismatic renewal, missional ecumenism, formal religious dialogues, and development of doctrines (especially since the Second Vatican Council) have all caused centuries of hostility to cool. But does this mean that the Reformation is now finished? With this question in view, we begin our first chapter with an examination of the lines of doctrinal agreement and difference between Catholics and Protestants.

CHAPTER 1

How Do the Fundamental Commitments of Catholics and Protestants Differ?

Catholic and Protestant teaching frequently suffers from selective quotation without regard to official documents and without taking into consideration how religious ideas influence the faithful. As it turns out, both doctrinal statements and personal piety are important when understanding each other. When our assessment sufficiently accounts for both, we begin to recognize how doctrinal beliefs are forged in the crucible of human experience and how they find expression through our neighbors, friends, and loved ones. Such a perspective does not simply enable us to engage religious ideas but also equips us to talk with people whose lives are committed to those ideas. This chapter will lay the groundwork for acquiring such a perspective.

One way to consider the important ideas and practices that distinguish Catholics and Protestants is to study the lives of thoughtful individuals who have converted from one side to the other. Such stories bring into focus the crucial turning points that lead a person toward or away from Rome.[1] They also tend to illustrate the enduring significance of the controversies from the sixteenth-century Reformation. Among the many outstanding examples of such conversion, the most notable is that of John Henry Newman (1801–1890), the Anglican turned Roman Catholic. Newman's journey of faith depicts the central issues that distinguish Catholics from Protestants. Furthermore, because it is impossible to understand contemporary Catholicism without some insight into Newman's thought, it is worth pausing for a moment to give him our attention.

It is sometimes overlooked that John Henry Newman started his religious journey as an evangelical. Under the tutelage of his Calvinist schoolmaster, the Rev. Walter Mayers, Newman experienced his first religious conversion (at the age of fifteen, between August and December of 1816). Mayers quickly became Newman's mentor, largely through giving Newman reading assignments. According to Newman, these lessons were "the human means of this beginning of divine faith in me" and "all of the school of Calvin."[2] It is noteworthy that while Newman's faith would move in different directions over his lifetime, he never repudiated his evangelical conversion.

As the years passed, Newman's religious curiosity caused him to rethink his ecclesial associations. On one hand, he sought to avoid the "high-and-dry" church (his way of describing religious liberals).[3] This was the arid and somewhat crusty church establishment that rejected the supernatural claims of Christianity. On the other hand, he grew to become increasingly troubled by Protestantism, which he found to be an overly fragmented and "emotional religion."[4] He was, however, not yet ready to become a Roman Catholic, which at this stage he regarded as overly superstitious. Therefore, Newman eventually pursued a middle course (*via media*) between evangelicalism and the Church of Rome in what came to be called the "Oxford Movement."

In September of 1833, Newman and his colleagues articulated their convictions in a series of articles titled *Tracts for the Times*. A primary target of the *Tracts* was the movement of Bible-centered evangelicals, which had grown exponentially throughout Britain. These were the folks about whom it would be said, "[It was] no written creed, no formal declaration of principles" that defined "Evangelical Religion."[5] With reference to these evangelicals, Newman and his colleagues exhibited a growing antipathy. He was therefore accused of having an agenda to undermine the Protestant character of the Church of England. Confronted by this concern, a friend warned that the Oxford *Tracts* "will be one day charged with rank Popery."[6] Evidently, John Henry's Rome-ward movement was becoming obvious.

The fundamental issue of importance, from Newman's perspective, was the status of religious authority and of the early church's dogmatic creeds, councils, and tradition. Due to suspicion or rejection of such theological sources by some of the Protestants whom Newman encountered, he saw evangelicalism as a boat tossed in a raging ocean of personal preference and subjectivity. From his point of view, this weakness was most clearly observed in the evangelical practice of private interpretation (the authority of believers to decide for themselves the meaning of Scripture), a concept that he regarded as absurd. In opposition to this practice, Newman preached a sermon expressing his frustration with the myriad of evangelical voices claiming to pronounce authoritatively on issues of doctrine. Instead of personal Bible study, Newman sought to fortify the church with a commitment to its ruling authority and liturgy.

Newman's attraction to Rome also led him to combat the Protestant doctrine of justification by faith alone (*sola fide*). Its tragic effect, as Newman saw it among evangelicals, was to reduce Christian faith to a subjective experience of conversion and to discard the need for obedience. In modern parlance we might call it "cheap grace." Therefore, instead of faith as the means by which one receives divine forgiveness, Newman pointed to the sacraments, which he regarded as comparatively more objective and reliable.

Before Newman's conscience would permit his conversion to the Roman Catholic Church, he had one more hesitation to overcome. Modern Catholicism, in Newman's view, appeared much different from the church of the early centuries, especially in reference to papal primacy. Newman eventually found a solution to this problem, proposing that external religious traditions grow into shape over time, like an acorn that develops into a tree. Similar to Charles Darwin's work, *On the Origin of Species*, Newman postulated his theory as an explanation of how a given subject may progressively develop into a new state. This enabled him to embrace the elements of Catholic tradition that lacked explicit testimony in the biblical text. Newman's classic book on the subject, *Essay on the Development of Doctrine*, was published in 1845 when he converted to the Catholic Church.

What can be learned from Newman's migration toward Rome? We might boil it down to two fundamental decisions—the first one concerns *authority*, and the second involves *salvation*. Concerning the former, he came to locate authority in the Church's hierarchy—an authority that came through apostolic succession, under whose authority doctrine develops. This ecclesial authority elevated tradition to the same level as Scripture as God's Word. On account of this, Newman emphasized the catechism and the creeds (where the church provides an authoritative interpretation of Scripture) as the sources to which Christians must look for religious instruction. Concerning the latter decision regarding salvation, Newman pointed to the grace of the sacraments (starting with grace's initiation in Baptism and continued in the Eucharist) as the way by which one is actually made righteous and accepted by God.

To be sure, the social and religious realities of Newman's

lifetime differed in many respects from the sixteenth century (and from the twenty-first). Nevertheless, the Reformation issues that distinguished Catholics and Protestants in his day still do so today. To better understand why these issues remain so intractable, let's take a closer look at some of the foundational concerns of these two respective traditions.

BY WHAT AUTHORITY?

It has been argued that the Catholic understanding of authority is best summarized by recognizing the interconnection of Christ and his Church,[7] the notion that the incarnated presence of Jesus is expressed in and through his Body. Thus, in the words of Father Richard John Neuhaus, "For the Catholic, faith in Christ and faith in the Church are one act of faith."[8] In this statement, Neuhaus echoes the *Catechism*: "Christ and his Church thus together make up the 'whole Christ' (*Christus totus*)" (CCC 795). Simply put, this type of "incarnation" is not simply a historical event from two millennia ago; it is the ongoing bond that makes the Church a single subject with Christ. Other ways of expressing this idea of the Church include the "continuing incarnation" and "the prolongation of Christ's mediatorial nature and work." As Pope Benedict XVI explained, "the Church [is] described as the Incarnation of the Son continuing until the end of time."[9]

Implications of the Christ-Church interconnection can hardly be overstated. It is, for instance, the reason why the Catholic Church understands itself to be the only valid and true Church, while Protestant assemblies are considered to be ecclesial communities, rather than actual churches. It is why Rome claims to be the determiner of the canon of Scripture. It is the basis of the Mass in which bread and wine become the actual body and blood of Christ and are therefore worshiped as divine (in Eucharistic adoration). It is why Catholicism mediates prayers, righteousness, and merits. And it is why evangelization (or ecumenism) for the Catholic Church is ultimately a matter of calling humanity home to Mother Church, which it regards as Christ in the world.

Protestants agree with Catholics that a vital union exists between Christ and his church. We stand together in affirming Christ is the Firstborn (Rom. 8:29), our Head (Eph. 4:15), the Branch into which we are grafted (Rom. 11:17). We agree that Christ is the eternal Word who speaks from his Church, resulting in a deeper experience of holiness and witness to the world. From a Protestant perspective, however, the Catholic concept of continuous incarnation—the notion that Christ's actual being, infallible revelation, and authority subsist in the one, holy, catholic, apostolic church—is inconsistent with Scripture. It is an infallible text that God gives us, not an infallible Church.[10] This conviction, that Scripture is the singular body of divine revelation and therefore the supreme authority, is captured by the Protestant phrase *sola scriptura*, "Scripture alone."

A helpful way to think about the concept of Scripture alone is in terms of the correlation between Jesus the *living* Word and Jesus' authoritative *written* Word (the Bible).[11] The inspired text is the way in which Jesus' revelation and authority extend to the church and the world.[12] In the words of Alister McGrath:

> When the first generation of Protestants spoke of the "author-
> ity of the Bible," this was to be understood as "the authority
> of the risen Christ, mediated and expressed through the
> Bible." . . . Precisely because Jesus Christ stands at the heart
> of the Christian faith, Protestants argue, so must the Bible.
> There is the most intimate interconnection between the Bible

and Christ in the Protestant tradition. The Bible is the means by which Christ is displayed, proclaimed, and manifested.[13]

Of particular importance to Protestants is what Scripture affirms for itself. For example, Paul says, "All Scripture is breathed out by God and profitable for teaching, for reproof, for correction, and for training in righteousness, that the man of God may be complete, equipped for every good work" (2 Tim. 3:16–17). Because this inspired Word sufficiently equips the church for every good work, Protestants seek to work out their salvation with explicit reference to it.

HOW SHALL WE BE SAVED?

There are several ways to compare the Catholic and Protestant doctrines of salvation. To begin with, we should recognize our common commitments.[14] We agree, for instance, that salvation is Trinitarian: The Father redeems sinful people and reconciles them to himself, through the work—the death and resurrection—and saving grace of Christ, by the regenerating work of the Holy Spirit. We believe that salvation is rooted in history, with implications that are spiritual, moral, relational, vocational, and more. We affirm that Jesus Christ, whose blood atones for our sins, has merited justification for us. And we recognize the aim of salvation to be the realization of holiness in service of the glory of God.

In addition to our similarities, we also have important differences. Our fundamental disagreement concerns the reason *why* God ultimately accepts sinful people. For Catholics, this acceptance is the culmination of a religious process, a faithful life nurtured by grace conveyed through the sacraments in which one grows in holiness. In the course of growing, one merits divine favor and, by doing so, eventually receives the divine declaration of acceptance. While the initial grace of salvation cannot be merited, faithful people merit for themselves and for others all the graces needed to obtain eternal life.

For Protestants, fallen humanity is unable to secure the smallest measure of divine merit by performing good works. Even the most selfless examples of human behavior are unworthy of God's favor. Instead, divine acceptance is based on the perfect righteousness of Christ, which is imputed (attributed or reckoned) to sinful people. In other words, because believers are "in Christ," clothed in his perfection, they are regarded by God as completely righteous. Unlike the Catholic system, in which the decisive verdict of God's acceptance follows a lifetime of accumulating sacramental grace in which one accrues merit (by performing good works), Protestants emphasize the decisive point when people believe in the gospel. At this moment of conversion, God accepts sinful people.

Once converted, children of God embark upon a journey toward holiness called the process of "sanctification." Regarding the necessity of this journey, Paul emphasizes: "But now he [God the Father] has reconciled you by Christ's physical body through death to present you holy in his sight, without blemish and free from accusation—*if you continue in your faith*, established and firm, and do not move from the hope held out in the gospel" (Col. 1:22–23 NIV, emphasis added). Paul's qualification is important to note: "if you continue in your faith." Evidently, this is what Newman failed to see among his evangelical contemporaries, leading him to regard their position as cheap grace. In fact, perseverance is necessary and will occur to authenticate the reality of one's faith. Those who do not persevere demonstrate they were not truly saved in the first place. For Protestants who don't have a Reformed outlook on salvation, such texts indicate that it is possible to lose salvation. In either instance, the Protestant vision insists that while justification is secured by faith alone, it is a faith that never remains alone because of ongoing sanctification by the transformative work of the Holy Spirit who lives within God's children.

At this point, a person might wonder, "Have not the differences of the sixteenth century concerning justification been resolved in the various ecumenical dialogues between Catholics and Protestants over the last fifty years?" What about the *Joint Declaration on the Doctrine of Justification* (*JD*) between the Lutheran World Federation and the Catholic Church, signed in Augsburg on October 31, 1999 (commemorating Luther's Ninety-Five Theses)? Having been formally accepted by the Catholic Church, it is recognized as "the most significant report" on justification.[15] The *JD* is also important for its stated goal of officially rescinding the mutual anathemas (condemnations of Protestants by Catholics, and of Catholics by Protestants) of the sixteenth century, that is, insofar as one accepts justification "presented in this *Declaration*."[16] Nevertheless, according to the *JD*, the sixteenth-century condemnations are to be taken seriously as "salutary warnings."[17]

So has the *JD* "closed the gap" between Catholics and Protestants on justification by withdrawing the anathemas? While Lutherans and Catholics may truly share the understanding presented in the Declaration, for non-Lutheran Protestants who do not embrace baptismal regeneration (the impartation of Christian life through the sacrament of baptism), the amount of shared understanding is comparatively modest. As for the question of whether Catholic teaching on the subject has developed or changed to the extent that it is now compatible with a Protestant understanding, historical theologian Anthony Lane responds: "No. When the difference in terminology is taken into account and when allowance is made for complementary formulations the gap turns out to be considerably narrower than is often popularly supposed, but a gap there remains."[18] Because the *JD* ignores the Protestant doctrine of the imputed righteousness of Christ and gives mere passing attention to issues such as purgatory and indulgences, its value should be assessed with sober judgment. Indeed, the Lutheran Church Missouri Synod (not a member of the Lutheran World Federation), denounced the *JD* as "a fraud and betrayal of the Gospel of our Lord Jesus Christ."[19] Accordingly, two fundamental issues—authority and salvation—are at the heart of the divide between Catholics and Protestants.

IS THE REFORMATION FINISHED?

Having identified these two fundamental differences between Catholics and Protestants, one might get the impression that not much has changed since the sixteenth-century Reformation. This would be a mistake. In the words of Mark Noll and Carolyn Nystrom, "Things are not the way they used to be."[20] Their assessment of contemporary Roman Catholicism traces the dramatic changes that have occurred since the Second Vatican Council (1962–1965). They point out the new ecumenical spirit, the increased importance on the role of the laity, the legacy of Pope John Paul II (updated to include the papacies of Benedict XVI and Francis), the changes in world Christianity, the burgeoning charismatic movement, and developments in American culture, including collaboration with evangelicals such as Billy Graham, initiatives such as Evangelicals and Catholics Together, and official Catholic-initiated dialogues with various Protestant groups. Noll and Nystrom conclude, "On the basis of the ecumenical dialogues, can it be said that the Reformation is over? Probably not. But a once-yawning chasm has certainly been narrowed."[21]

Using the theological ideals of the Reformation to assess

contemporary Catholicism, Noll and Nystrom underscore the chief areas of Catholic disagreement with Protestantism. These include the use of Scripture, the nature of Christ's presence in the Mass, justification by faith, and a litany of other subjects including the papacy, magisterium, Mary, the sacraments, and mandatory priestly celibacy. However, underlying all of this diversity, "the central difference that continues to separate evangelicals and Catholics, is . . . the nature of the church."[22] This is still the case because the Catholic Church regards itself as Christ on earth with divine authority to forgive sins and impart sanctifying grace. Again, we see how the Christ-Church interconnection is a basic distinction between Catholics and Protestants.

The work of Noll and Nystrom is meticulously researched, documented, and engagingly applied. It is therefore regrettable that they stopped short of providing an explicit answer to the question of the book, *Is the Reformation Over?* Instead, the authors chose to be evasive:

Yet asking whether the Reformation is over may not even be the most pertinent question. It may be more to the point to ask other questions: Is God truly going to draw people from every tribe and tongue and people and nation—and major Christian tradition—to worship together the Lamb who was slain? Can he really make of them—all these tongues and peoples and traditions—a single kingdom united in the body of his Son Jesus Christ? Should believers in an all-powerful, all-merciful God doubt that such signs and wonders might still take place?[23]

Catholics and Protestants alike share these concerns. Our Lord Jesus Christ, in his high priestly prayer (John 17), underscores the priority of Christian unity, and the apostle Paul exhorts the church to earnestly preserve it (Eph. 4:3). At the same time, we must be prepared to give an answer for the gospel-centered hope within us. With our calling to proclaim the good news in this historical moment, to make disciples of all nations, to shepherd families suffering from relational fallout (even between Catholic and Protestant relatives), and to uphold righteousness in our increasingly decadent society, doctrinal clarity is of crucial importance. With this in mind, in chapter 2 we'll take a close look at the ways Catholics and Protestants continue to stand together and where they stand apart.

CHAPTER 2

Where Protestants and Catholics Stand Together

Ten Commonalities

Despite objections to the contrary—objections that are often voiced heatedly and emphatically by rabid anti-Catholic Protestants and rabid anti-Protestant Catholics—there are many essential beliefs that unite the Catholic and Protestant traditions. These commonalities reflect the major themes of Scripture, the core doctrines formulated by the early church councils and expressed in early creeds (e.g., the Nicene-Constantinopolitan Creed, the Apostles' Creed), and beliefs that were assumed from the beginning and communicated in the church's worship services, sermons, catechisms, and writings.

THE TRIUNE GOD

We begin by noting that Protestants and Catholics agree on the doctrine of the Trinity. "Trinity" refers to the triunity, or three-in-oneness of God: he eternally exists as Father, Son, and Holy Spirit. Each of these three persons is fully God, sharing alike in the one divine nature. The Father is fully God. The Son is fully God. The

Holy Spirit is fully God. They are alike in every way in terms of their divine attributes and glory.

Though equal in nature, they are distinct persons: The Father is not the Son and not the Holy Spirit. The Son is not the Father and not the Holy Spirit. The Holy Spirit is not the Father and not the Son. The three are distinguishable by their different eternal relationships and by their different roles in creation, salvation, and sanctification. Their eternal relationships (often called relations of origin) differentiate each of them.

(1) The Father is characterized by *paternity*: he is eternally the Father of the Son. He relates as Father to the Son by loving him, giving him all things (e.g., his name, glory, words, and works), and sending him to become the incarnate God-man, Jesus Christ.

(2) The Son is characterized by *eternal generation*: the Father eternally generates (or begets) the Son, meaning that he grants to the Son his sonship, or life-as-the-Son. Thus, the Son is eternally generated (or begotten) of the Father. This does not mean that the Father grants deity to the Son, for the Son is God-of-himself. It also does not mean that the Father is superior to the Son, or that the Son is inferior to the Father. Rather, they are equal in every way in their divine nature.

(3) The Holy Spirit is characterized by *eternal procession*: the Father and the Son eternally spirate[1] the Holy Spirit, meaning that they grant to the Spirit his life-as-the-Spirit. Thus, the Spirit eternally proceeds from both the Father and the Son. This does not mean that the Father and the Son grant deity to the Spirit, for the Spirit is God-of-himself. It also does not mean that the Father and the Son are superior to the Spirit, or that the Spirit is inferior to the Father and the Son. Rather, they are equal in every way in their divine nature.

These eternal relationships distinguish the three persons. On this important belief, Eastern Orthodoxy disagrees with Catholicism and Protestantism. It holds that the Holy Spirit proceeds from the Father alone, not from the Father and the Son. But Protestants and Catholics have strong biblical support for their common view of the eternal procession of the Holy Spirit from the Father and the Son.[2]

Note their prominent roles, by which the three persons are also distinguished:

(1) The Father plays the primary role in *creation*, speaking the universe and everything that it contains into existence. Still, the Son as the agent of creation and the Spirit as preparer and perfector of creation also participate in creation.

(2) The Son plays the primary role in *salvation*, becoming incarnate, living a holy life, dying, resurrecting, and ascending. Still, the Father as the one who sent the Son and the Spirit as the one who applies salvation participate in salvation as well.

(3) The Holy Spirit plays the primary role in *sanctification*, being the one who transforms Christians into the image of Christ. Still, the Father who brings Christians to glory and the Son who develops Christians in holiness also participate in sanctification. These roles in creation, salvation, and sanctification distinguish the three persons.

Though eternally existing as Father, Son, and Holy Spirit—three distinct persons in terms of their relationships and roles—there is only one God. Protestants and Catholics are not tritheists, believing in three gods. Rather, they are monotheists, believing in one God who is triune. They worship the triune God—eternally existing as Father, Son, and Holy Spirit—as the one, true, and living God.

THE NATURE OF GOD

Catholics and Protestants generally agree on the nature of this tri-une God, affirming the following divine attributes in accordance with God's own revelation of himself:[3]

Independence: God is self-existent; indeed, his very nature is to exist. Independence is the opposite of dependence or contingency, which is true of all created things. God is not dependent, and he cannot be dependent on anything or anyone else.

Immutability: God is unchanging, the same yesterday, today, and forever. God is immutable in his (1) triune nature; (2) attributes, as presented in this section; (3) plan, that is, his purpose for all creation that he is bringing to pass; and (4) promises, all that he pledges to be and do for his people.

Eternity: God always exists, not being bound by time. He has no beginning; God has always existed. He has no end; God will always exist. And God does not develop presently in terms of time-sequence. Indeed, God existed before time, which he created when he made the universe.

Spirituality/Invisibility: God is an invisible, spiritual being, not composed of any material element. Because of God's spiritual nature, no one has ever seen, or can see, God.

Omnipresence: God is present everywhere, not being bound by space. Furthermore, it is not as though part of God is present in one place and another part in another place. Rather, God is present everywhere with his whole being at the same time.

Omnipotence: God is all-powerful. He is able to do everything that is fitting for him as God to do. This means (thankfully) there are some things—for example, breaking his promises, ceasing to be God, sinning, lying—that God cannot do.

Omniscience: God is all-knowing. He fully knows himself, the past, the present, the future, the decisions and actions of his creatures, all actual things, and all possible things. God does not grow in knowledge by learning new things.

Wisdom: God always wills the highest purposes and the proper means to achieve those purposes for his own glory and his people's blessing. Divine wisdom is clearly seen in creation, salvation, and the church.

Truthfulness and Faithfulness: God always tells the truth and always fulfills his promises. Indeed, he cannot lie and cannot be unfaithful to his word.

Love: God always gives of himself. Love eternally characterizes the Father, Son, and Holy Spirit. From this trinitarian love flows the creation of the world, which God continues to love even when it is hostile toward him. Indeed, God's love is demonstrated in the sending of his Son to die for sinful people.

Goodness/Grace/Mercy/Patience: God is kind and benevolent. He is good in and of himself, and all his ways in creation, providence, and salvation are good. In grace, God expresses his goodness to people who deserve condemnation. In mercy, God expresses his goodness to people who are distressed. In patience, God expresses his goodness by withholding punishment.

Holiness: God is both exalted above creation and absolutely morally pure. Because of his transcendent holiness, God is completely separated from his creation. Because of his moral holiness, God is completely pure and uncorrupted by sin.

Righteousness/Justice: God is upright in himself and in his ways. God himself is absolutely righteous and acts in ways that are perfect. He is just in establishing moral standards, requiring conformity to them, and judging people's obedience and disobedience.

Jealousy: God is protective of his honor. Because he alone is God, only he is worthy of ultimate allegiance. Thus, when people, who were created to honor God, honor something or someone else, God is provoked to jealousy.

Wrath: God intensely hates sin and is ready to punish it fully. Because he is holy, God cannot approve anything that is not perfectly holy. Because he is righteous, God metes out punishment against anything that violates his right standards.

Glory: God is infinitely beautiful because of who he is. This beauty is displayed as God manifests himself in creation, redemption, and consummation. Glory is also the magnificent splendor that shines from the revelation of God and his ways.

Though these divine attributes may be named and defined in different ways, Catholics and Protestants acknowledge them as the characteristics of God.

THE REVELATION OF GOD

Protestants and Catholics affirm the existence of God, who is knowable through both general and special revelation. Indeed, if people ask how we know that God is triune in nature and characterized by the attributes presented above, Catholics and Protestants alike point to God's disclosure of himself through revelation.

One means of such divine self-disclosure is *general revelation*, or God's communication of himself to all people at all times and in all places. General revelation comes in four modes: (1) *creation*, which displays God's eternal power and divine nature; (2) *the human conscience*, which presents basic principles of right and wrong; (3) *God's providential care*, which manifests his kindness and goodness for his created people; and (4) *an innate sense of God*, a hard-wiring with an intuitive awareness of him. To this list Catholics and some Protestants add *proofs for God's existence*. These rational evidences include *cosmological and teleological arguments*, taking as their starting point the world (*cosmos*) and its design or purpose (*telos*) as proof that God exists. Additionally, *moral and aesthetic arguments* take as their starting point the universal sense of morality, beauty, and the search for happiness as proof of God's existence.

Through general revelation, all people at all times and in all places know that God exists, some of his divine attributes (power, goodness, kindness), and basic principles of right and wrong (preserving life is right, murder is wrong). Whereas Catholics believe that God "can be known with certainty from the created world by the natural light of human reason" (CCC 36), Protestants are typically more skeptical toward general revelation's ability to dispose people to faith. The problem does not lie with the revelation itself, which does indeed supply knowledge of God. Rather, the sinfulness of people distorts their perception of such revelation, rendering it unfruitful. Thus, both Protestants and Catholics agree on the insufficiency of general revelation to establish a personal relationship between God and his people. Indeed, another kind of revelation is needed for such intimacy with God.

This mode is *special/divine revelation,*[4] or God's particular communication of himself to particular people at particular times and in particular places. Divine revelation, realized in deeds and words that are closely tied together (CCC 53), comes in various modes: (1) *the mighty acts of God,* like the crossing of the Red Sea and Jesus' miracles; (2) *dreams and visions,* like Isaiah's image of the holy God; (3) *direct divine speech,* like God's call of Abraham and his giving of the Ten Commandments; (4) *the incarnation* of the Son of God as Jesus Christ by which God himself became a man; and (5) *inspired communication.*

On this last mode, Catholics and Protestants affirm together that Scripture is the God-breathed, written revelation of God. A major point of departure, however, comes at this point: Protestants, following the Reformation principle of *sola Scriptura*, affirm that Scripture, and Scripture alone, is the ultimate authority. Catholics reject this principle and insist that divine revelation is transmitted by a twofold pattern of *written Scripture and oral Tradition*.[5] More will be said about this major difference later. Still, we note that although they differ on the role of Tradition, Protestants and Catholics both highlight the transformative power of Scripture and its centrality for salvation, Christian living, and worship.

A final point of agreement: Catholics and Protestants affirm the human ability to speak about God. Such ability is not exhaustive and faultless: human speech about God cannot be comprehensive and perfect. But it is adequate and true speech. In support of this affirmation, Catholics underscore the *analogy of being*: because of a resemblance between finite people, who are created in the divine image, and the infinite God who created them in his image, language about God is possible. Though many Protestants do not appeal to the analogy of being, they still support the adequacy of human speech about God in other ways.[6] For example, they point to God's creation of human speech, the incarnate Son's use of common human language in his ministry, and the Holy Spirit's inspiration of Scripture in common human languages (Hebrew, Aramaic, Greek) as arguments which support the truth that human language is sufficient to speak about God.

THE PERSON OF JESUS CHRIST

Catholics and Protestants also have widespread agreement concerning the identity of the second person of the Trinity and his incarnation as the God-man Jesus Christ. These commonalities are:

Trinitarian relationships: The Son of God eternally exists as the second person of the triune God. Generated by the Father, he is the son yet still deity. Together with the Father, the Son eternally spirates the Holy Spirit so that the Spirit proceeds from both the Father and the Son.

Incarnation: According to the eternal plan of the Godhead, the Son willingly became incarnate about two thousand years ago. Indeed, Jesus Christ "was conceived by the Holy Spirit, [and] born of the Virgin Mary" (Apostles' Creed). Mary was a young teenage girl who, betrothed to Joseph, had never engaged in sexual intercourse with him (or with any other man, for that matter). As announced by the angel Gabriel, Mary the virgin became pregnant through the productive power of the Holy Spirit. Thus, she "conceive[d] the eternal Son of the Father in a humanity drawn from her own" (CCC 485).

Fully divine nature: The resulting God-man was fully divine. He did not set aside any of the divine attributes that he eternally shared together with the Father and the Holy Spirit. He continued to be omnipresent, omnipotent, omniscient, eternal, and so forth. As the saying goes, "remaining what he was, he became what he had never been." In other words, the incarnate Son remained fully divine while taking on human nature as never before.

Fully human nature: The resulting God-man was fully human. He had a human mind, human feelings, human will, human motivations, human purposing, and a human body. In his intellect, emotions, will, drives, aims, and body, Jesus Christ was the same as all other human beings, with the exception of sin. He was not a superman, sliding through life without care or confronting temptations and trials with supernatural powers. On the contrary, his birth and development physically, intellectually, spiritually, and socially were like all other human beings. He was hungry and needed food for nourishment. He was thirsty and needed water to quench his thirstiness. He was tired and needed to rest and sleep.

He suffered horrifically the excruciating pain of betrayal, denial, beatings, public nakedness, mockery, and crucifixion. He was fully human.

One person, two natures: In the incarnation, the God-man was one person with two complete natures. Catholics and Protestants alike denounce historical heresies such as:

(1) *Docetism*: Jesus Christ only seemed to be a human being, but was not.

(2) *Arianism*: Jesus Christ was a created being—the first to be created, the highest to be created, and the one through whom everything else was created—and, as a created being, was not eternal nor of the same nature as the Father.

(3) *Nestorianism*: The divine person of the Son of God joined with the human person of Jesus Christ, two persons dwelling in cooperation within one man.

(4) *Eutychianism* or *monophysitism*:[7] The divine person of the Son absorbed the human nature so that Jesus Christ was a DIVINEhuman being; or, the divine and human natures fused together to form a hybrid, dhiuvmianne being.

(5) *Apollinarianism*: Jesus Christ was partially human, possessing a human body, but he was not fully human, lacking a human soul. He was essentially a divine soul plugged into a human body.

The early church councils and their creeds—the Council of Nicea and its Creed of Nicea (325); the First Council of Constantinople and its Nicene-Constantinopolitan Creed (381); the Council of Ephesus (431); and the Council of Chalcedon and its Chalcedonian Creed (451)—refuted these heresies and formulated sound Christological doctrine. Later councils advanced this doctrine: The person who was crucified was identical to the second person of the Trinity (Second Council of Constantinople, 553). And Jesus Christ had two wills (*dythelitism*), one divine, one human, thus denying the one will doctrine of *monothelitism* (Third Council of Constantinople, 680/681).[8]

Both Catholics and Protestants embrace this classical Christology.

THE SAVING WORK OF CHRIST

Protestants and Catholics are united in their doctrine of the work of Jesus Christ to accomplish salvation for sinful people. The common elements include:

Christ's Sufferings

Throughout his earthly ministry, Jesus suffered in ways that are common to human beings. For example, he faced many temptations, and these were not confined to his trials in the wilderness at the hand of Satan (Matt. 4:1–11). He experienced misunderstanding. For example, his family imagined that he was insane (Mark 3:20–21). He knew persecution by enemies. For example, the religious leaders thought he was both insane and possessed by the devil (John 10:20). He was incensed at the ugly specter of death and the havoc that it wreaked (John 11:33), and the hardness of people's hearts infuriated him (Mark 3:4–5). His own closest friends never grasped his full identity and purpose (Mark 8:14–21). Indeed, Judas betrayed him (Matt. 26:14–16, 47–50), and Peter denied ever knowing him (Luke 22:34, 54–62).

Though Christ encountered these miseries that are common to humanity, his sufferings went beyond the normal human experience. First, Jesus provoked many of these trials by challenging the Jewish religion and leadership of his day. Specifically, he called into question the popular understanding of the law, the temple, and faith (CCC 574–591). Second, his sufferings were salvific in nature: every trial and persecution that he faced contributed to his redemptive work on behalf of sinful people. Indeed, "Although he was a son, he learned obedience through what he suffered. And being made perfect, he became the source of eternal salvation to all who obey him" (Heb. 5:8–9). Mysteriously, the holy Son of God, incarnate as the sinless Jesus Christ, was prepared through suffering for the ultimate sacrifice that he would offer in order to save sinful people.

Christ's Crucifixion

Christ's highest act of obedience was voiced in the Garden of Gethsemane and carried out at the crucifixion. "Father, if you are willing, remove this cup from me. Nevertheless, not my will, but yours, be done" (Luke 22:42). As just noted, he was well prepared for this ultimate act of obedience, and it was completely in step with Jesus' constant obedience throughout his life.

Jesus' crucifixion "was not the result of chance in an unfortunate coincidence of circumstances" (CCC 599). Rather, he was "delivered up according to the definite plan and foreknowledge of God" (Acts 2:23). The guilty co-conspirators enacted exactly what God's hand and plan "had predestined to take place" (Acts 4:28). On the human level, Jesus was crucified because he confronted the religious establishment and political powers of his day. But according to his own testimony, for the sake of sinful people like those who crucified him, Christ came "to give his life as a ransom for many" (Matt. 20:28).

Christ's Atoning Sacrifice

A ransom in Jesus' day was the price paid to redeem, or buy out, helpless people from a slave market. As a striking image of what Christ's death achieved, *redemption* is one aspect of his atoning sacrifice. A second picture is that of *propitiation*: Christ's death assuaged the furious wrath of God against sin. A third image is that of *expiation*: Christ's death removed the liability to suffer punishment because of sin and guilt. A final figure is that of *reconciliation*: Christ's death removed the enmity between God and sinful people and restored the two parties to friendship. These four images present the multi-sided nature of Christ's atoning sacrifice: As the substitute for sinful people, Jesus paid the penalty of sin in their place, for their sake. His atonement accomplished the forgiveness of their sins, their justification, their salvation.

Because of a common Protestant misunderstanding of Catholic doctrine of the atonement, it must be underscored that Catholics do not believe that Christ is re-sacrificed each and every time the Catholic Church celebrates the sacrament of the Eucharist. Catholics and Protestants alike acknowledge that Christ was crucified once on the cross. His sacrifice is once-for-all-time. As Scripture announces: "And every priest [under the old covenant] stands daily at his service, offering repeatedly the same sacrifices, which can never take away sins. But when Christ had offered for all time a single sacrifice for sins, he sat down at the right hand of God" (Heb. 10:11–12). The sufferings, crucifixion, and atoning sacrifice of Christ accomplished salvation for sinful people.

This doctrine of Jesus Christ finds widespread agreement among Protestants and Catholics.

THE HOLY SPIRIT

Additionally, Catholics and Protestants are in full accord with regard to the identity of the third person of the Trinity. They also share a number of commonalities with respect to his work.

Trinitarian relationships: The Holy Spirit eternally exists as the third person of the triune God. He proceeds from the Father and the Son. They sent the Spirit on the day of Pentecost to launch his new covenant ministry. Together with them, the Spirit is worshiped and glorified.

Name and titles: The proper name of the third person is "the Holy Spirit." His titles include "Paraclete," the helper/counselor/ advocate; "the Spirit of truth"; "the Spirit of promise"; "the Spirit of adoption"; "the good Spirit"; and "the Spirit of glory." He is "the Spirit of God/the Lord" (the Father) and "the Spirit of Christ" (the Son).

His deity: Two parallel statements by Peter in dealing with the grievous sin of Ananias and Sapphira highlight the deity of the Holy Spirit. The apostle charged that Ananias had "lied to *the Holy Spirit*" and that he has "not lied to man but *to God*" (Acts 5:3–4, emphasis added). A bit later Peter confronts Sapphira, questioning how Ananias and she "have agreed together to test the Spirit of the Lord" (Acts 5:9). "To test the Spirit of the Lord" is an Old Testament expression for sinning against God (e.g., Exod. 17:1–2; Deut. 6:16). The deity of the Holy Spirit is also demonstrated by his divine attributes—omnipresence, omniscience, omnipotence, eternality, and the like—and his divine works in creation, salvation, and consummation.

His works prior to Christ's coming: The Holy Spirit was active in the creation, hovering over the chaotic waters of the newly created world. He was protecting and preparing it for God's work of rendering it a place that would be hospitable for human beings. With respect to the people of God, the Holy Spirit stirred up judges and empowered them to deliver Israel from its oppressors. He came upon the kings of Israel and equipped them to rule. The Spirit spoke by the mouths of the prophets. What is more, these prophets announced the coming of Messiah, a new covenant, and a fresh, new, unprecedented outpouring of the Holy Spirit.

His works in relation to Christ's coming: The Virgin Mary conceived Jesus Christ through the overshadowing of the Holy Spirit (Luke 1:35: Matt. 1:18–25). John the Baptist, who was filled with the Spirit from his mother's womb, baptized with water. But he announced that Messiah would baptize with the Holy Spirit (Luke 3:15–17). When John baptized Jesus as Jesus entered into his Messianic ministry, the Father spoke words of commendation to the Son and the Holy Spirit descended upon him like a dove (Luke 3:21–22). It was this Spirit who empowered Jesus throughout his ministry (Luke 4:1, 14; Acts 10:38). Though he was filled with the Holy Spirit without measure, Jesus anticipated a fresh, new, unprecedented outpouring of the Spirit on his followers. This promise was fulfilled on the day of Pentecost.

His works in relation to salvation: The Holy Spirit is active in applying salvation. According to John 16:8–11, he convicts the world—people who are hostile toward God—of sin (especially unbelief), self-righteousness (reliance on one's works to merit God's favor), and worldly judgment (evaluation of others by mere appearance). He is the one who regenerates these sin-conscious people, removing their old sinful nature and replacing it with a new nature (John 3:3–5; Titus 3:5–6). The Spirit enables people to proclaim "Jesus is Lord" (1 Cor. 12:1–3). He seals these believers, guaranteeing the fullness of their salvation in the future (2 Cor. 1:22), and he grants them assurance of their inheritance (Rom. 8:16–17). As the primary agent in sanctification, the Spirit produces Christ-likeness (Gal. 5:22–23). Other works of the Holy Spirit include prayer for Christians, illumination of Scripture, spiritual gifts, guidance, unity in the church, and the establishment of leaders. Clearly, Catholics and Protestants have many points in common regarding the Holy Spirit.

THE GLORY AND TRAVESTY OF HUMAN BEINGS

Protestants and Catholics have substantial overlap with respect to the doctrines of humanity and sin. Especially important are their common views regarding creation in the image of God, the human constitution, Adam and Eve, and original sin.

Image of God

At the apex of his creative work, God deliberated within himself: "Let us make man in our image, after our likeness" (Gen. 1:26). Thus, he created human beings as male image bearers and female image bearers (Gen. 1:27). To them he gave the responsibility to reflect and represent him: "Be fruitful and multiply and fill the earth and subdue it, and have dominion. . . ." (Gen. 1:28). All human beings are created in the divine image; such creation gives them dignity and significance. It also enables them "to know and love" their Creator (CCC 356). Because of the unity of the human race in its creation, all people everywhere should express love and solidarity for one another. Also, a fundamental identity of the image of God is maleness and femaleness: God's image bearers are either male or female, and genderedness is an essential identity of human beings. Men and women alike are created in the divine image, meaning that they are equal in terms of personhood, dignity, and significance.

Human Constitution

Creation in the divine image means that a person is a complex being: He consists of both a material element, or body, and an immaterial element, or soul/spirit. Catholics and many Protestants understand this immaterial aspect to be the inner core of what it means to be human. Indeed, the soul is considered to be a person's most important part, "that by which he is most especially in God's image" (CCC 363).[9] This focus should not be taken to ignore or belittle the material aspect, for the "human body shares in the dignity of 'the image of God'" (CCC 364).[10] Accordingly, Catholics and most Protestants hold to *dichotomy*: human beings consist of two parts, body and soul/spirit. Some Protestants, however, hold to *trichotomy*: the human constitution consists of three parts, body, soul, and spirit.[11]

Adam and Eve

The original image bearers were Adam and Eve. God created them as upright people: they imaged God obediently and faithfully. Their original state was one of holiness and righteousness. Accordingly, integrity characterized their relationship with God: they enjoyed a personal, face-to-face relationship with him unclouded by sin, guilt, and shame. And they lived without the fear of death and punishment. Moreover, Adam and Eve were persons of integrity, without any tendency to sin. Furthermore, they experienced harmony in their relationship with one another: they were naked and unashamed (Gen. 2:25), totally transparent with each other. And they lived in a pristine environment, in a garden that was lush and fertile and in which they exercised dominion. Indeed, they had everything that they needed, living in a world that God himself had assessed as "very good" (Gen. 1:31).

Tragically, Adam and Eve did not maintain their original integrity. Wrestling with the divine prohibition regarding the tree of the knowledge of good and evil (Gen. 2:16–17), they disobeyed God (Gen. 3:1–7). Their once face-to-face relationship with God was broken; they now feared him. Such spiritual death, or alienation from God, was part of the threat with which God had warned them. Personally, they experienced a corruption of their nature. Relationally, the original soundness of their rapport soured into lust, tension, power grabbing, and harsh domination. Environmentally, their initial harmony with creation turned into dissonance: Procreation of new life would now be characterized by suffering. Vocation would take on a painful and toilsome character. Moreover, their existence would one day come to an end, as physical death was introduced as divine punishment for their sin (Gen. 3:16–19).

Original Sin

As if the devastating results of Adam and Eve's sin on them were not enough, the travesty of the fall is that its consequences were not confined only to them. Rather, sin spread universally (Rom. 5:12–21). Every person who comes into this world is implicated in this sin. Original sin, as it is known, is transmitted to everyone. It is the state into which everyone is born, consisting of guilt before God and corruption of human nature. This original sin is the source of all acts of sin, for which people are guilty before God and therefore in need of salvation.

Though Catholics and Protestants agree on these broad strokes of the doctrines of humanity and sin, many points of difference separate them, which will be taken up later.

SALVATION IS INITIATED BY GOD

Catholics and Protestants agree that the initiative in salvation lies completely with God. This divine initiative applies both to the accomplishment of salvation and to the appropriation of salvation.

Divine Initiative in Accomplishing Salvation

Although the saving work of Christ was treated earlier, that section focused on his atoning sacrifice by crucifixion. Certainly, Jesus' death is at the heart of the accomplishment of salvation, but more needs to be said. From all eternity, the triune God purposed to provide redemption for the people he would one day create and permit to fall. Indeed, Christ as the sacrificial lamb "was foreknown before the foundation of the world" (1 Pet. 1:19–20). Thus, the rescue scheme for sinful people was part of the eternal plan of God. Clearly, no human being contributed to this strategy; it was wholly divine.

At the right time and in the right place, the enactment of that plan began to unfold, again through divine initiative: "But when the fullness of time had come, God sent forth his Son, born of woman, born under the law, to redeem those who were under the law, so that we might receive adoption as sons" (Gal. 4:4–5). As Jesus himself emphasized, it was God the Father who sent him to be the savior of humanity: "For I have come down from heaven, not to do my own will but the will of him who sent me" (John 6:38). For this task, Jesus was empowered by the Holy Spirit, in fulfillment of Old Testament prophecy: "The Spirit of the Lord is upon me, because he has anointed me to proclaim good news to the poor." (Luke 4:18). As the anointed Messiah sent by the Father, Jesus "through the eternal Spirit offered himself without blemish to God" (Heb. 9:14). Having accomplished redemption, the crucified Savior rose from the dead three days later through the power of the Father and the Holy Spirit. This collaborative work of the triune God underscores the divine initiative in accomplishing salvation for sinful people.

Divine Initiative in Applying Salvation

As with the accomplishment of salvation, so also with its application: the experience of salvation comes about through divine initiative.[12] It begins in eternity past, as the Father "chose us in him [Christ] before the foundation of the world, that we should be holy and blameless before him" (Eph. 1:4). Moreover, this "holy calling [was] not because of our works but because of his own purpose and grace, which he gave us in Christ Jesus" (2 Tim. 1:9). God's choice was not because of something inherent in us and not on the basis of our meritorious good deeds but according to his gracious purpose alone. The application of salvation continues as the Father draws people to Jesus (John 6:44), Jesus chooses them (and not the other way around; John 15:16), and, through Jesus, people come to the Father (John 14:6). This divine action does not overlook or deny the proper and necessary human decision to repent of sin and express faith in Christ for salvation to take place. But God's grace prompts faith (Acts 18:27) and is at the heart of salvation: "For by grace you have been saved through faith. And this is not your own doing; it is the gift of God, not a result of works, so that no one may boast" (Eph. 2:8–9). The application of salvation comes at divine initiative.

This divine initiative is confirmed in regard to one of the key points separating Catholics and Protestants: justification. Protestants may be surprised to learn that Catholic theology denies any role for human initiative and merit at the outset of salvation. Rather, its beginning depends solely on the grace of God: "No one can merit the initial grace of forgiveness and justification" (CCC 2010).

Salvation is a gracious, divine work, and God takes the initiative in accomplishing and applying it, an understanding both Catholics and Protestants affirm.

GOD MAKES US HIS PEOPLE

You may be surprised to learn that Protestants and Catholics also have some commonalities with respect to the people of God, that is, the doctrine of the church. These agreements are the biblical images for God's people, the four attributes of the church, and the purposes for which the church exists. At the same time, while Catholics and Protestants present these points using similar language, they often have different nuances and definitions of them.

Scripture portrays the church as the people of God, the body of Christ, and the temple of the Holy Spirit. As the people of God, members of the church have been chosen and saved by him. Thus, they stand apart from the world. Catholics and many Protestants would add that as the people of God, Christians are a priestly, prophetic, and royal people: they exercise the three roles of Jesus Christ as priests, prophets, and kings. Speaking of Christ, Paul affirms that God "put all things under his feet and gave him as head over all things to the church, which is his body, the fullness of him who fills all in all" (Eph. 1:22–23). As cosmic head over all created things, Christ is the head of the church, which is his body, living in faith and obedience to him through the Holy Spirit. It is the Spirit who makes and dwells in his temple, which is the church (1 Cor. 3:16). Indeed, people from every walk of life "are being built together into a dwelling place for God by the Spirit" (Eph. 2:22). Catholics and Protestants agree that the church is the people of God, the body of Christ, and the temple of the Holy Spirit—an agreement that is based on these images being found in Scripture. At the same time, the two traditions understand these images in very different ways.

A second commonality is the four classical identity markers ascribed to the church: *oneness* (or unity), *holiness*, *catholicity* (or universality), and *apostolicity*. The church is *one* because of (1) its source, the triune God; (2) its Savior, the incarnate Son; and (3) the indwelling presence of the Holy Spirit, who is also the foundation of its unity (Eph. 4:3). The church is *holy* because of God's gracious gift of purity that, while real, is imperfect. The church makes progress in holiness as God sanctifies it, making it more fully conformed to the image of Christ. The church is *catholic*, or universal, in accordance with Jesus' Great Commission (Matt. 28:18–20). He does not allow his church to be limited in its scope. Rather, Christ's love controls the church, compelling it to be missional in reaching out to all people everywhere (2 Cor. 5:14–21). Finally, the church is *apostolic*, or founded on the apostles of Jesus Christ (Eph. 2:20) and responsible to transmit the "good deposit" (2 Tim. 1:13–14), or sound doctrine. Still, while Catholics and most Protestants embrace this four-fold characterization of the church, their concepts of oneness, holiness, catholicity, and apostolicity, while possessing some overlap, are significantly different. And Protestants will also emphasize additional marks of the true church: the preaching of the Word of God, the administration of the sacraments, and (for some) the exercise of church discipline. Catholics, while also incorporating these elements, do not consider them to be marks of the true church.

A final commonality is found in the church's purposes. The church exists (1) to worship God, that is, give him the honor and glory that is due to him; (2) to build up Christians, aiding them to increase in holiness so as to please God and experience his blessing; and (3) to engage non-Christians with the gospel, that is, to be missionally involved in evangelism/evangelization of those who do not yet know Christ as Savior. At the heart of the church's life and mission are the sacraments or ordinances. These rites communicate or express in concrete form the grace of God to the church. While disagreeing on many aspects of the sacraments, Catholics and Protestants alike practice baptism and the Lord's Supper.

THE LIVING HOPE

Catholics and Protestants enjoy broad agreement on many points concerning the living hope to which they are called, or the doctrine of the future. These agreements fall into two general categories: personal hope and cosmic hope.

The personal hope shared in common focuses on Jesus Christ, who has overcome death, which is the penalty for sin. Because all people have sinned, they are destined to face divine judgment. The hope is that through Christ's saving work, by which he paid the penalty for sin, people who embrace his merciful provision will escape eternal condemnation and enjoy eternal life instead. Thus, there are two eternal destinies: *Eternal condemnation* is the future of all who fail to repent of their sin and accept the love of God in Christ. *Eternal life* is the other destiny. Though Catholics and Protestants agree with this future, a major point of division concerns how sinful people may enjoy eternal life (a point to be discussed later). Furthermore, while agreeing that there are two eternal destinies, Catholics differentiate themselves from Protestants by holding to a *temporary destiny* after death, which is *purgatory* (also to be discussed later).

Broader consensus is found when we turn to the cosmic hope of God's people. This hope again focuses on Jesus Christ, but it is now directed to his bodily return, or second coming to earth. This forthcoming event has been determined by God but cannot be known by any human being (Mark 13:32). Whereas his first coming was in a state of humiliation and suffering, Christ's second coming will be characterized by great power and glory. The resurrection of the body, for both the good and the wicked, will accompany Christ's return. Both the resurrected righteous and the resurrected unrighteous will appear before Christ at his judgment seat. He will mete out the last judgment. The eternal destinies already dispensed at the individual judgment at death will now be put on public display: the wicked "will go away into eternal punishment, but the righteous into eternal life" (Matt. 25:46).

For Catholics and some Protestants, Christ's second coming and last judgment will bring to an end this present, earthly age, and it will introduce the age to come, that is, the new heaven and new earth. Other Protestants believe that between the second coming of Christ and the renewal of the universe will be a period of time called the millennium. As he returns from heaven to earth, Christ will establish his kingdom, his physical reign over this world that will last for a thousand years.[13] At the end of this millennium age, Christ will decisively defeat one final, last-ditch effort by Satan and his evil forces. Christ's cosmic victory will initiate the renewal of all creation in the new heaven and new earth.

Accordingly, the ultimate future hope is the re-creation of all that exists. The now fallen creation, which suffers as the result of human sinfulness, will be gloriously renewed (Rom. 8:18–23). All existence will be united in Christ (Eph. 1:10). The church, portrayed as "the Bride, the wife of the Lamb" (Rev. 21:9), becomes the New Jerusalem, and God will dwell forever among his people. And God and his people will eternally live in glory and blessedness in the new heaven and new earth.

Catholics and Protestants share much in common about their future hope.

These ten essential beliefs constitute the common ground on which Protestants and Catholics stand together. In the next two chapters, we'll take a closer look at the key differences between what Catholics believe and what most Protestants believe.

CHAPTER 3

Key Differences between Protestants and Catholics (Part 1)

Scripture, Tradition, and Interpretation

Having presented the common ground on which Protestants and Catholics stand together, we can now look at the major points of division that continue to separate these two traditions. To unpack these differences, we will ask several questions. Catholics and Protestants each provide distinct answers to these questions, and their answers on these issues reflect the key points of difference between them.

HOW DOES GOD SPEAK TO THE WORLD?

Earlier, we noted that Protestants and Catholics stand together in affirming that God reveals himself to the world through both general and special revelation. Through general revelation, all people at all times and in all places know that God exists, some of his divine attributes, and basic principles of right and wrong. Because of human sinfulness, however, general revelation is insufficient to establish a personal relationship between God and his people. Special revelation (called "divine revelation" by Catholic theology) is needed for such intimacy with God. How does God speak to the world through such revelation? A major difference between Catholics and Protestants is found in the answer to this question.

Catholics affirm that God speaks to the world through Tradition and Scripture. Similar to the twofold way that Jesus' apostles communicated the gospel—*orally*, through preaching, and *in writing*, through the biblical text—so God communicates to his people today in a twofold pattern: the teaching, or *Tradition*, of the Church's bishops, who are the successors of the apostles, and *Scripture*. "Sacred Tradition and Sacred Scripture are bound closely together and communicate one with the other. For both of them, flowing out of the same divine well-spring, come together in some fashion to form one thing and move toward the same goal" (CCC 80). Thus, these two modes are two streams of one source of divine authority.

Tradition is "the Word of God which has been entrusted to the apostles by Christ the Lord and the Holy Spirit" (CCC 81). This oral communication was in turn handed over by the apostles to their successors, the bishops of the Church, who maintain this Tradition and, on occasion, proclaim it as Church doctrine. For example, the Church declares the immaculate conception of Mary and her bodily assumption (to be treated later) as part of Tradition. The other mode of divine revelation is Scripture. Though Catholics and Protestants stand together in their belief that the Bible is the God-breathed, written revelation of God, they part company on many other points in their understanding of Scripture. Significantly, the Catholic Church "does not derive her certainty about all revealed truths from the holy Scriptures alone. Both Scripture and Tradition must be accepted and honored with equal sentiments of devotion and reverence" (CCC 82).

Against the Catholic affirmation of Scripture and Tradition as authoritative divine revelation, Protestants assert the principle of *sola Scriptura*: Scripture, and Scripture alone, is authoritative divine revelation. God speaks to the world through his Word, which is written Scripture only, not Scripture plus Tradition. This Protestant critique of Tradition is grounded on several points.

First, Protestants believe that the Catholic position has thin biblical support. For example, to buttress their position, Catholics appeal to Jesus' explanation to his disciples: "I still have many things to say to you, but you cannot bear them now" (John 16:12). They claim this passage as an example of Jesus underscoring the necessity of both Scripture and Tradition—what he could reveal to them as he was speaking with them, and what he would need to reveal to them later, when they were able to absorb it.

The Protestant response insists that this interpretation misses the point of that interaction. It is simply telling us that as Jesus was speaking with his disciples, they could not grasp his revelation— what he was saying to them at that moment. Indeed, in short order, they would express utter confusion about his impending death (John 16:16–24). Even when they thought they could understand the unfolding calamity, Jesus informed them that they would all abandon him (John 16:25–33), and soon afterward devil-prompted Judas was poised to betray him (John 13:2; 18:1–8), and Peter denied ever knowing Jesus (John 18:15–18, 25–27).

Following Jesus' crucifixion and resurrection, however, the disciples received the Holy Spirit. As Jesus had promised, the Spirit taught the disciples all things, brought to their remembrance all that Jesus had said to them, and guided them into all the truth (John 14:26; 16:13). Having removed the prior dullness and ignorance that had characterized the disciples, the Holy Spirit moved those who wrote Scripture to communicate the whole of divine revelation (our New Testament). This work was exactly what Jesus taught about his sending the Holy Spirit to inspire them to write Scripture. Protestants believe that, understood in context, there was no need for supplemental communication—Tradition—alongside of Scripture.[1]

Second, Protestants believe that the Catholic view has thin historical support as well. It is true that the apostles communicated the gospel both orally, through their preaching, and eventually in writing, through the New Testament. But when Paul points out "so then, brothers, stand firm and hold to the traditions that you were taught by us, either by our spoken word or by our letter" (2 Thess. 2:15), he is not saying that his oral teaching and his written communication consisted of different revelations which supplement each other. On the contrary, these two delivery systems presented the same divine revelation. The difference was in the form, not the content.

The early church did have a type of tradition: the doctrine that the apostles transmitted provided a proper understanding of Scripture and underscored sound doctrine. It stood in opposition to the wrong biblical interpretations of the time and the misguided beliefs of heretics. The early church's "rule of faith" or "canon (standard) of truth" was a summary of its essential doctrines based on Scripture. The early creeds—for example, the Apostles' Creed and the Chalcedonian Creed—affirmed the doctrines of the Trinity and of Christ derived very carefully from Scripture. Protestants embrace *this* type of tradition, finding it to be a fine source of wisdom from the past. But this is far from the Catholic notion of Tradition.

In fact, it was not until the fourteenth century that the Catholic Church began to make novel claims about Tradition, granting unwritten communication by Church leaders authoritative status as doctrine outside of, and in addition to, Scripture. Such an idea of

Tradition is a relatively late development and is quite different from the notion as found in Scripture and in the early church.[2]

Standing opposed to the Catholic view of Scripture and Tradition as two modes of divine revelation, Protestants hold to the *sufficiency* and *necessity* of Scripture. Scripture is sufficient in that it provides everything that people need to be saved from sin and death, and everything that Christians need to please God fully. Specifically, God-breathed Scripture equips believers "for every good work" (2 Tim. 3:16–17). Protestants see doctrines like the immaculate conception and bodily assumption of Mary as unnecessary and unbiblical. Protestants don't need these doctrines to possess and believe the fullness of divine revelation. They don't need practices like the sacrament of penance and praying for the dead in order to know and do all that God requires of them. They don't need to believe that when they take the Lord's Supper, the bread and the wine are transubstantiated into the body and blood of Christ. These doctrines, practices, and beliefs are extra-biblical, not from Scripture alone. Thus, Scripture's sufficiency and the principle of *sola Scriptura*—"Scripture alone"—are closely connected and contradict the need for Catholic Tradition.[3]

Scripture is necessary in that it is essential for knowing the way of salvation, for progressing in godliness, and for understanding God's will. To put it another way, apart from Scripture there can be no awareness of salvation, growth in holiness, and knowledge of God's will.[4] Catholics, on the other hand, would maintain that Scripture is necessary for the *well-being* of the Church: for the Church to be robustly all that God intends it to be, Scripture is necessary. But Catholics would not hold that Scripture is necessary for the *being* of the Church: if Scripture were to be lost, the Church could still exist because it would still have Tradition, part of divine revelation. Protestants insist that the Church would lose its way without Scripture: if Scripture were to be lost, the Church would cease to exist because all of divine revelation would have disappeared.

How does God speak to the world? Catholics respond to this question by saying "through Scripture and Tradition." Protestants reply, "through Scripture alone."

TO WHAT EXTENT IS GOD'S WORD WITHOUT ERROR?

If we dialed back the clock two hundred years, all Catholics and Protestants would express belief in the *truthfulness* of all of Scripture. This attribute means that everything Scripture affirms is true. Another way of stating this is to acknowledge the inerrancy of Scripture: it does not contain any errors. Scripture's affirmation of divine creation out of nothing, its narration of the events surrounding the exodus of Israel out of Egypt, and its rehearsal of Israel's sin and divine judgment in terms of the captivities—these affirmations are true. Likewise, its fourfold account of the life and ministry of Jesus of Nazareth as the Son of God incarnate, its stories of his miraculous acts including feeding the five thousand and raising Lazarus from the dead, its explanation of Christ's death as the work of the God-man sacrificing himself to pay the penalty for sin as the substitute for sinful people, and its chronicles of the founding and expansion of the early church—these affirmations are true. All that Scripture affirms corresponds to reality, and it never contradicts itself. With a few rare exceptions, Protestants and Catholics alike assumed and, if necessary, defended the full truthfulness and inerrancy of Scripture.

This crucial doctrine of Scripture was the legacy they received from the Jewish people's high view of the Hebrew Bible, mediated through the early church. In turn, the early church handed down this conviction to the medieval church, which then passed it off to the Catholic Church and the Protestant churches at the time of the Reformation and in the post-Reformation period. An example of the church's historical position on Scripture comes from Augustine:

> I have learned to yield this respect and honor only to the canonical books of Scripture: of these alone do I most firmly believe that the authors were completely free from error. And if in these writings I am perplexed by anything which appears to me opposed to truth, I do not hesitate to suppose that either the manuscript is faulty or the translator has not caught the meaning of what was said, or I myself have failed to understand it.[5]

In the seventeenth and eighteenth centuries, a new, critical attitude toward Scripture developed, calling into question the inerrancy and truthfulness of the Bible. Yet even with the beginning and development of biblical criticism in these centuries, doubts about or dismissals of Scripture's truthfulness were still quite rare. The belief in the inerrancy of Scripture remained a fixture for both Protestants and Catholics until the nineteenth century when the historic position of the church began to unravel.

Protestant liberalism led the way in undercutting belief in Scripture's inerrancy. The Catholic Church (rightly) denounced this Protestant liberal innovation and cautioned Catholic scholars who would dare embrace it. Sadly, Catholic biblical scholarship, infected by the Protestant liberalism of that era, began to weaken on this issue in the first half of the twentieth century. Protestant liberalism itself was countered by movements like fundamentalism and evangelicalism, conservative Protestant movements that affirmed biblical inerrancy throughout the twentieth century. During this time, the majority of Catholics maintained a conservative position as well.

A watershed moment took place during the Catholic Church's Vatican Council II (1962–1965). During their work in committee on what would later become *Dei Verbum: The Dogmatic Constitution on Divine Revelation*, the bishops and cardinals originally wrote drafts setting forth a conservative view on inerrancy. One draft affirmed that Scripture is "completely free from all error," while another draft declared that it "teaches the truth without error." These statements were met with opposition from Cardinal Franz König of Vienna, who insisted that the Church *could not* affirm the inerrancy of all Scripture because of the presence of actual errors in it.[6] Cardinal König's intervention stirred up a great deal of controversy, as he and other contributors to the final draft of *Dei Verbum* lobbied for a doctrinal statement that would emphasize the inspiration of Scripture yet limit the scope of its inerrancy.

In the end, the Council adopted a statement that is considered by some Catholics to be ambiguous on the issue of Scripture's truthfulness. And despite attempts by other contributors, and Pope Paul VI himself, to avoid such ambiguity, the final draft (*Dei Verbum* 11) affirms:

> Therefore, since everything asserted by the inspired authors or sacred writers must be held to be asserted by the Holy Spirit, it follows that the books of Scripture must be acknowledged as teaching solidly, faithfully and without error that truth which God wanted put into sacred writings *for the sake of salvation* [emphasis added].

The italicized phrase "for the sake of salvation" is the phrase that was in dispute. Non-inerrantists point to it as limiting the scope of inerrancy to biblical passages that address matters of salvation, faith, morals, and the like. In support of their interpretation, they reference the historical development behind this statement, which we rehearsed above.[7] Inerrantists deny that the phrase materially limits the scope of inerrancy; indeed, they insist it *cannot* be read in any way that affirms limited inerrancy. In support, they note the affirmation in the first part of the sentence that "everything asserted" by the biblical authors "must be held to be asserted by the Holy Spirit." And because the Holy Spirit cannot assert anything that is in error but only that which is true, neither can the biblical writers assert anything that is in error but only that which is true. Inerrantists also point to the section's footnotes, which reference Augustine (including his *Letter 82*, cited above) and several other authorities that uphold the inerrancy of all Scripture.[8]

Still, it is most accurate to acknowledge that Catholics are divided on the issue of Scripture's inerrancy. And so, too, are Protestants. Still, we should recognize that one of the hallmarks of evangelical Protestantism is a commitment to the truthfulness of all Scripture. This is clearly seen in the movement's *Chicago Statement on Biblical Inerrancy*. According to one of its short statements, "Being wholly and verbally God-given, Scripture is without error or fault in all its teachings, no less in what it states about God's act in creation, about the events of world history, and about its own literary origins under God, than in its witness to God's saving grace in individual lives." Among its articles of affirmation and denial, article 12 states: "WE AFFIRM that Scripture in its entirety is inerrant, being free from all falsehood, fraud, or deceit. WE DENY that biblical infallibility and inerrancy are limited to spiritual, religious, or redemptive themes, exclusive of assertions in the fields of history and science." Further evidence for inerrancy as a characteristic feature of evangelical Protestantism is the statement of faith of the Evangelical Theological Society. Besides belief in the Trinity, ETS is centered on only one other doctrine: "The Bible alone, and the Bible in its entirety, is the Word of God written and is therefore inerrant in the autographs."

To what extent, then, is God's Word without error? Without minimizing the commitment of many Catholics to the truthfulness of all Scripture, it is fair to conclude that the doctrine of biblical inerrancy is not a hallmark of their faith, at least not to the same extent that it is with evangelical Protestants. Catholics who champion this belief certainly stand together with evangelical Protestants; yet tragically, it is a doctrine that is increasingly surrendered by many Catholics and liberal Protestants today.

OF WHAT DOES THE BIBLE CONSIST?

If we look at the Catholic Bible and the Protestant Bible from a distance, they appear nearly identical. The New Testament of both Bibles is exactly the same. So is the vast majority of the Old Testament. Yet notice the exception in that statement. For while we can say that the vast majority of the Old Testament is the same, *not all is the same*, and this difference is a major point of division between the two traditions. The Catholic version of the Old Testament consists of several more writings than does its Protestant counterpart.

Specifically, the canon (the list of books that belong to) of the Catholic version of the Old Testament includes the *apocryphal writings*, or the *Apocrypha* for short. These extra books are: Tobit, Judith, the Wisdom of Solomon, Ecclesiasticus,[9] Baruch, 1 and 2 Maccabees, additions to Esther, and additions to Daniel. The word *apocryphal* signifies "hidden," but we are not sure exactly why this word became attached to these extra Old Testament writings.

Historically, the Hebrew Bible, which was the sacred book of the Jews, consisted of the following writings, divided into three divisions:[10]

- *The Law*: Genesis, Exodus, Leviticus, Numbers, and Deuteronomy
- *The Prophets*: Joshua, Judges, Ruth, 1 Samuel, 2 Samuel, 1 Kings, 2 Kings, Jeremiah, Lamentations, Ezekiel, Isaiah, Hosea, Joel, Amos, Obadiah, Jonah, Micah, Nahum, Habakkuk, Zephaniah, Haggai, Zechariah, Malachi, Job, Daniel, Ezra, Nehemiah, 1 Chronicles, 2 Chronicles, Esther
- *The Writings*: Psalms, Proverbs, Ecclesiastes, Song of Songs

Note that the Hebrew Bible did not include any of the apocryphal writings. Because Jesus was a Palestinian Jew, these are the writings that would have been included in the Bible that he used. Indeed, when he stood up to read in the synagogue in Nazareth, "the scroll of the prophet Isaiah" that was handed to him (Luke 4:17) was written in Hebrew and was a part of this Hebrew Bible.

Before the time of Christ, Jews that had been forcibly ejected from their homeland had ended up living in places where Greek was spoken, written, and read. Greek versions of the Hebrew Bible were prepared for them so that they could have Scripture in their new language. The most noted of these Greek translations is called the Septuagint, or LXX for short.[11] It is this version of the Hebrew Bible, a Greek translation, that contained the additional apocryphal writings.[12] As the early Christian church expanded from its roots in Jerusalem into the Greek-speaking Gentile world, the Septuagint naturally became its Old Testament.

At the same time, the earliest historical evidence available to us decidedly supports the view that the early Christian church matched its canonical Old Testament Scriptures to correspond to the writings found in the Hebrew Bible—*not the Greek translation*. That is, the early church was decidedly against viewing the apocryphal writings as being part of authoritative, God-breathed Scripture. Church leaders like Melito of Sardis, Origen, and Athanasius composed lists of the church's Old Testament, and the books that they included were the same as, or very similar to, the writings in the Hebrew Bible. They also explicitly noted that many of the apocryphal writings were *not* canonical. And while these early church leaders wrote commentaries on all the Old Testament books, they did not do so with the apocryphal books.

Beginning in the second century after Christ, the common language of the world in which Christianity was expanding changed to Latin. To continue to make the Scriptures accessible to those speaking Latin, the church began to translate its Bible, which consisted of the Old Testament and the emerging New Testament, into Latin. The Old Testament of the first Latin Bibles was translated not from Hebrew but from the Septuagint. Thus, the early Latin Bibles naturally included the additional apocryphal writings.

In 382, Jerome (345–420) was commissioned to make a new translation of the Bible. Being an excellent Hebrew scholar, he began his translation of the Old Testament by working from the original Hebrew Bible. He composed a list of the canonical Old Testament Scripture, including only the writings found in the Hebrew Bible. For Jerome, these alone were truly Scripture, as he underscored: "what is not found in our list must be placed among the apocryphal writings."[13] These non-canonical books were Wisdom of Solomon, Ecclesiasticus, Judith, Tobit, and 1 and 2 Maccabees. Still, he did not altogether dismiss these writings. Making an important distinction, Jerome encouraged the church to read them "for the edification of the people, not to give authority to doctrines of the church."[14] Reading these apocryphal books, with their many stories of courage, hope, obedience, faithfulness, and perseverance in persecution, contributes to the church's maturity. However, using them for establishing or defining doctrine is prohibited.

Augustine (354–430), a contemporary and friend of Jerome, exerted a powerful influence on the translation work that Jerome did. Augustine was convinced that the Holy Spirit had been at work in both the authors of the Hebrew Bible and the translators of the Septuagint. He believed this to be the case because the apostles, writing the New Testament in Greek, quoted both the Hebrew Bible (with their citations rendered into Greek) and the Septuagint. If the apostles considered that both the Hebrew Bible and the Septuagint should be used as authoritative because both are God-breathed, then Augustine and the church should adopt that same apostolic attitude toward them. Accordingly, Augustine prevailed upon Jerome to include Latin translations of the apocryphal writings in Jerome's Latin *Vulgate*. This translation, with its additional books in the Old Testament, was approved by regional church councils and became the official Bible of the church.

The church's reliance upon the Latin Vulgate continued without significant challenge for over a thousand years until the sixteenth century. At that time, the Protestant Reformers, starting with Martin Luther, called into question the canonicity of the apocryphal writings. They argued that these writings had never been part of the Hebrew Bible. They had not been part of the Bible used by Jesus. No New Testament author had quoted from any of the apocryphal writings. They had not been considered canonical by the early church. Some of them contained historical and chronological errors. So, following Jerome's distinction, the Reformers agreed that the church could read the Apocrypha for its progress in holiness but could not appeal to it to establish doctrine.

The Catholic Church replied decisively to this Protestant dismissal of the Apocrypha. At its Council of Trent (1546), the Church proclaimed, "If anyone does not receive, as sacred and canonical, these books, with all their parts, as they have been read in the Catholic Church and as they are contained in the old Latin Vulgate edition, and knowingly and deliberately rejects the above mentioned traditions, let him be anathema [cursed]."[15] In saying this, the Catholic Church determined what it considered to be the canon of Scripture and its authoritative version.

What difference does this disagreement about Scripture's canon make for us today? One example is the doctrine of purgatory and the practice of praying for the dead. Catholic support for this doctrine focuses primarily on a passage in 2 Maccabees (12:38–45; see later discussion). Yet because Protestants do not believe 2 Maccabees to be part of authoritative, God-breathed Scripture, they do not believe in purgatory nor practice praying for the dead.

What difference does the disagreement Catholics and Protestants have about Scripture's language make? Consider the Catholic belief in the sacrament of penance. As quoted above, the official Catholic version of Scripture is the Latin Vulgate. Its rendition of Jesus' words in Matthew 4:17 *Poenitentiam agite* can be translated "do [acts of] penance." The Greek New Testament, however, has *metanoeite*, that is, "repent." The original Greek tells us that Jesus did not command his followers to engage in the sacrament of penance but to change their heart and life.

Purgatory. Prayer for the dead. The sacrament of penance. These are major points of division between Catholics and Protestants, and they all stem from their use of different Bibles.

Of what does the Bible consist, then? Catholics respond, "the Old Testament, including the Apocrypha, and the New Testament, specifically the Latin Vulgate." Protestants reply, "the

Old Testament, without the Apocrypha, and the New Testament." There are clear differences between the two.

HOW ARE WE TO UNDERSTAND THE WORD OF GOD?

It is one matter to possess the Word of God. You can own a Bible. But it is another matter—and a necessary step—to interpret it so as to understand what God is speaking to the world. Two diverse answers to the question "How are Christians to understand the Word of God?" highlight yet another key difference between Catholics and Protestants. Catholics point to their Church's hierarchy to render the official interpretation of the Word of God. Protestants point to the clarity of Scripture that enables all believers, under the illumination of the Holy Spirit, the guidance of pastors and teachers, and principles of sound interpretation, to understand God's Word.

As we have seen, Catholics consider the Word of God to consist of both Scripture and Tradition. There are two modes of divine revelation, and both must be interpreted. Catholics believe that "the task of giving an authentic interpretation of the Word of God, whether in its written form or in the form of Tradition, has been entrusted to the living teaching office of the Church alone" (CCC 85). This teaching office, composed of the pope and the bishops, is called the Magisterium. The right to interpret Scripture and Tradition has been given to the Magisterium. This means that the Magisterium—the pope and the bishops of the Catholic Church—possesses the authority to declare doctrines, like the immaculate conception and the bodily assumption of Mary, that are binding on all Catholics. It also means that all Catholic interpretations of Scripture must conform to the Magisterium's interpretation. Even more fundamentally, this means that the Catholic Church has a threefold "structure of authority: written Scripture, Tradition, and the Magisterium. Just as the three poles of a three-legged stool provide support for whoever sits on it, these three elements provide divine revelation and its authoritative interpretation for the Church."[16]

As noted earlier, Protestants do not consider Tradition to be a mode of the Word of God. Scripture, and Scripture only, constitutes God's Word. Furthermore, they do not have a Magisterium. Certainly, some Protestant churches and denominations have authoritative governing structures (for example, synods or national assemblies) above the local church level. These higher-level bodies, however, do not function like, nor do they possess the authority of, the Catholic Church's Magisterium. They do not claim to exercise the right to determine the authoritative interpretation of Scripture. Indeed, all Protestants decry the Magisterium's pretension as authoritative interpreter of Scripture. They also point to its wrong biblical interpretations as evidence against its claim.

Does this mean that Protestants are consigned to interpretive chaos, with no hope of ever having a valid interpretation of Scripture? Does their rejection of the Catholic Magisterium mean that Protestants are abandoned to interpretive relativism in which biblical passages mean whatever any individual Protestant wants them to mean? Certainly not. Protestants champion the *clarity* of Scripture: it is written in such a way that it is understandable for Christians. As they are illumined by the Holy Spirit, Christians have the ability and the responsibility to interpret the Bible. Possessing the attribute of clarity, "Scripture itself is characterized by the presumption of continued intelligibility; that is, it assumes that when the Word of God is read/heard, even in contexts far removed from the original settings in which it was written, people will comprehend it."[17]

Moreover, Protestant churches are led by pastors (also called elders) who have the responsibility to preach and teach the Word of God. Additionally, the Holy Spirit gives the gift of teaching to some church members. Pastors and gifted teachers bear the responsibility of helping their congregation to understand properly and practically the Word of God. Thus, each Protestant church has a teaching office or ministry to which members give heed.

Another major difference between Catholics and Protestants is their understanding of what constitutes the meaning of Scripture. For Catholics, Scripture has multiple senses, which become a fourfold meaning: The foundational sense is (1) the *literal sense*, or the meaning of the words—phrases, sentences, narratives, poems, etc.—of Scripture. From this literal sense come the *spiritual senses*, or the meanings of the things—people, events, institutions— about which Scripture speaks. This spiritual sense consists of three meanings: (2) the *allegorical sense*, or the Christological meaning; (3) the *tropological sense*, or the meaning for Christian conduct; and (4) the *anagogical sense*, or the meaning in terms of its future fulfillment. For Catholics, most if not all biblical passages contain these multiple senses, and the task of interpreters is to discern these various meanings, and all interpretations must submit to the authoritative interpretation of the Magisterium.

Protestants historically have rejected this fourfold meaning of Scripture.[18] For example, Martin Luther championed the "literal," or "grammatical, historical meaning" to understanding the Bible.[19] Thus, biblical interpretation pays close attention to the *grammar* of the text: the meaning and function of words, the connection of words and phrases, the genre or literary type, the flow of narratives, the figurative language of poems, and the like. Biblical interpretation also considers carefully the *historical context* of the text: the cultural background of the time that the text was written, its author and original recipients, its purpose, and more. This grammatical-historical approach emphasizes the intention of the biblical author/Author as key to proper interpretation.

The *redemptive-historical context* of the text is especially important to note: its place in the progress of revelation, its connection to earlier and later passages, its relation to the biblical covenants, and the like. Because Christ is the center of all Scripture, biblical interpretation should seek to understand what it "drives home" about Christ.[20] Protestant interpretation also embraces *typology*. Typology notes the author's intended relationships between earlier *types*—people (Moses), places (the temple), institutions (the sacrificial system), and things (the bronze serpent)—and their later *antitypes*, especially Christ and his sacrificial death on the cross.[21] Other key principles include the need to interpret Scripture (1) with attention to its whole context, (2) in light of the historic Christian faith or sound doctrine (the "analogy of faith"), and (3) with dependence on the illumination of the Holy Spirit.

Importantly, we should mention that the Catholic Church *does* encourage the application of similar principles to biblical interpretation: the intention of the biblical author/Author as expressed in words, the grammar and historical context, the genre, the whole of Scripture, in harmony with the Holy Spirit, and so forth (CCC 109–110). Happily, the Church also fosters the reading and studying of Scripture by promoting easy access to it. Indeed, the Church highlights Jerome's words: "Ignorance of the Scriptures is ignorance of Christ" (CCC 133).

And yet, Catholics are not known for their personal Bible reading and community Bible studies, whereas such engagement with Scripture is a hallmark of Protestants, especially evangelical Protestants. Indeed, it has only been in the last fifty years since Vatican Council II that the Catholic Church has strongly encouraged the ministry of the Word. This emphasis is seen particularly in its worship services (the Liturgy of the Word is the first part of the Catholic mass), its preaching (the homilies in the mass should be based on the liturgical readings from the Old Testament, the New Testament, and the Gospels), and its catechesis (the teaching of the faith to Catholic laity).

In addition, the vast majority of Bible translation work worldwide has been and is carried out by Protestant groups. Historically, the Catholic Church has, at times, condemned translations of the Bible into the common languages of the people (for example, John Wycliffe's English Bible was banned in 1408). The Protestant Reformation, fueled by the clarity, sufficiency, and necessity of Scripture, produced Bible translations in German, French, Czech, Polish, English, and other languages. The contemporary push for translation—currently, over five hundred of the complete Bible—into all languages in the world comes largely from Protestants. The importance of this task is to render the Bible accessible in the language of the people so that they may read and study it, interpret and understand it, as is their responsibility before God.

How are we to understand the Word of God? Catholics respond, "with dependence on, and in accordance with, the Magisterium's official interpretation." Protestants reply, "with the illumination of the Holy Spirit, knowing that Scripture is clear, following sound interpretive principles, and with the help of their pastors."

CHAPTER 4

Key Differences between Protestants and Catholics (Part 2)

Image of God, Sin, and Mary

WHAT DOES IT MEAN TO BE MADE IN THE IMAGE OF GOD?

Catholics and Protestants enjoy broad agreement on the glory and value of human beings. Often we talk about this in reference to what it means to be made in the image of God. Here, the two traditions agree on numerous points. Catholics and Protestants agree that creation in the divine image is unique to human beings and enables people to enjoy a personal relationship with God. Our creation in the image of God involves our genderedness as either male or female, with the corollary that men and women are equal in terms of personhood and stewardship. Indeed, being in the image of God entails the responsibility of both genders to reflect and represent God, especially in relation to procreation and vocation. It is the source of human dignity and significance. Creation in the image of God, being true of all human beings, is the ground of the expression of human love for, and solidarity with, one another.

A major point of difference, however, appears in the two traditions' view of the original state of Adam and Eve. Protestants and

Catholics agree that God created these first two human beings as upright people: they imaged God obediently and faithfully. Their original state was one of holiness and righteousness. But Catholics believe that Adam's soul and Eve's soul governed their passions and body. That is, the first couple's reason or rationality—their intellectual capacity—ruled their appetite for food and drink, their feelings of love and esteem, their will to depend and be grateful, their motivations for achievement and significance, their desire for sexual intercourse, and the like.

A key support for this view is the traditional distinction Catholics make between the *image* of God—his natural gifts of reason and free will—and the *likeness* of God—the supernatural gifts of original holiness and immortality. This distinction comes from the divine deliberation: "Let us make man in our image, after our likeness" (Gen. 1:26). According to the Catholic interpretation, when God created Adam and Eve, he gave them natural gifts: the image of God, that is, rationality and freedom. And he gave them supernatural gifts: the likeness of God, that is, righteousness and everlasting life. Thus, Catholics closely associate, if not identify, the divine image with human reason. Another support to which Catholics point is the vast historical precedence for their view, beginning with early church leaders who held this position.

Protestants, in growing number, dissent from this near identification of the image of God with human reason. And while many Protestants have historically followed Catholics in maintaining this viewpoint, advances in contemporary scholarship have led to a careful reconsideration of this traditional view. Specifically, linguistics has overwhelmingly demonstrated the error in making a sharp distinction between the image of God and the likeness of God. In the biblical texts, these terms are synonyms and are used interchangeably.[1] Accordingly, the Catholic distinction between natural gifts (the image of God) and supernatural gifts (the likeness of God) cannot be sustained from a linguistic standpoint. And this means that the identification of the image of God with human rationality cannot be maintained either. Old Testament scholarship has also demonstrated that the emphasis on creation in the divine image in Genesis 1 is on the human function of exercising dominion over the rest of the created order, not the possession of rational abilities.

Rather than illegitimately restricting the divine image to one aspect or characteristic of human nature (an intellectual capacity, as Catholics understand it), being created in God's image/likeness should be understood to refer to human beings in their wholeness. People are made in the divine image as holistic human beings consisting of reason/intellect, emotions and attitudes, a will, a body, moral capabilities, motivations and purposing, relationships, activities, and the like. God created human beings in their wholeness to be his image bearers. As Chris Rice sings it,

> Lying on pillows we're haunted and half-awake
> Does anyone hear us pray, "If I die before I wake"
> Then the morning comes and the mirror's the other place
> Where we wrestle face to face with the image of Deity
> The image of Deity.[2]

To look in the mirror is to see the image of God, not to be found merely in an attribute like reason or a capacity such as the intellect but as a human being in his or her totality. The traditional Catholic (and at times Protestant) limitation of the divine image to human rationality is obsolete today.

A second major point of difference flows from this first one. Whereas Catholics imagine that there was a potential inner struggle within Adam and Eve as they were originally created, Protestants disagree. According to Catholics, the potential inner struggle existed between the original couple's soul—that is, their reason or intellect—and their passions and body. They believe that this latent instability was divinely designed. That is, God created Adam and Eve in this way. While characterized by integrity, in the original state in which they were created, Adam and Eve were given a super-natural gift of righteousness—part of their creation in the likeness of God. By means of this special gift, their rationality controlled their appetites, desires, and bodily yearnings. Yet when they fell from this state of integrity, Adam and Eve lost their original right-eousness and the instability within them reared its ugly head: their passions and bodily cravings usurped their reason and wreaked internal havoc. We'll unpack more about their fall into sin later.

At this point, though, we would simply point out that Protestants disagree with this portrait of the original state of Adam and Eve. Scripture gives no hint of such a latent instability kept in check by a supernatural gift of righteousness. On the contrary, the biblical account focuses on their creation as being actualized exactly according to plan:

> Then God said, "Let us make man in our image, after our likeness. And let them have dominion over the fish of the sea and over the birds of the heavens and over the livestock and over all the earth and over every creeping thing that creeps on the earth."
>
> > So God created man in his own image,
> > in the image of God he created him;
> > male and female he created them.
>
> (Gen. 1:26–27)

First came the divine plan, and then God executed it by creating Adam and Eve according to his intention. Next he blessed them, and he gave them the responsibility to exercise dominion over the rest of creation, according to his intention (Gen. 1:28). As he had done previously, God rendered his assessment of the now completed creation, with one twist: instead of the divine pronouncement being it was "good" (Gen. 1:4, 10, 12, 18, 21, 25), it becomes it was "very good" (v. 31). Adam and Eve were image bearers made in accordance with the divine plan. As created beings they lived in a creation that was divinely assessed as "very good." In summary, Adam and Eve were *not* characterized by some kind of potential inner struggle with their soul governing their passions and body by means of supernatural righteousness.

What does it mean to be made in the image of God? Catholics respond, "the divine gift of human reason, which rules over the passions and the body by means of a supernatural gift of righteousness." Protestants reply, "human beings in their wholeness without a hint of potential inner struggle kept in check by a special gift."

WHAT IS SIN AND ITS CONSEQUENCES?

As discussed earlier, several commonalities are found between Catholics and Protestants regarding the doctrine of sin. Both traditions agree that sin is a violation of God's law, an offense against God, a failure to love God and other human beings, rebellion against God's will, and much more. Both concur that the sin of Adam and Eve wreaked havoc with their relationships with God, themselves, and the rest of creation. Both traditions agree that because of the fall, sin and its consequences spread to the entire human race that would come from them (Rom. 5:12–21). Both affirm that original sin is the condition into which every person is born, bringing guilt before God and corruption of human nature.

Beyond these points of commonality, however, several key differences appear. First, Catholics make a distinction between mortal and venial sins. A *mortal sin* is a serious violation of God's law. It is committed with full knowledge of its wrongness and with complete consent, being a deliberate and free choice to sin. Mortal sin destroys love and forfeits grace. If not forgiven through the sacrament of Penance, mortal sin results in eternal condemnation in hell. *Venial sin* is a less serious matter. It may involve a lesser violation of God's law. Or it may be a serious violation but committed without full knowledge or full consent. Venial sin wounds love in one's heart but does not destroy it. It impedes progress in doing good but does not forfeit grace. While not resulting in eternal condemnation, venial sin does merit temporal punishment in purgatory. Confession and repentance, but not the sacrament of Penance, repairs venial sin.

Protestants do not make these distinctions and do not distinguish between mortal and venial sins. Yes, Scripture makes a distinction between unintentional and intentional sins (Num. 15:27–31). Moreover, some sins are more serious (murder, immorality), while other sins are less serious (spreading rumors, harboring resentment). But despite differences in gravity and consequences, all sins incur guilt before God (James 2:10–11; Gal. 3:10). Each and every sin brings divine judgment of eternal condemnation. Accordingly, the idea that mortal sins incur greater guilt while venial sins incur lesser guilt—thus, not resulting in divine judgment of eternal condemnation—does not square with Scripture. Thus, the Catholic distinction between mortal and venial sins is incorrect.

A second difference regards original sin. The Catholic view builds on the belief, discussed above, that the fall resulted in a loss of supernatural righteousness with a consequent disruption of the soul's (or reason's) governance of the passions and body. Adam and Eve became dominated by their lower nature. The same is now true of all human beings born with original sin: their lower, emotional and physical nature illegitimately dominates their higher, intellectual nature. This Catholic view of the original state of Adam and Eve, who, as divinely-designed, were characterized by a latent instability within them, has been critiqued. The corollary of that view—that the same disruption of reason's ruling position by the passions and body characterizes all human beings through original sin—is consequently wrong as well. While affirming the corruption of human nature, Catholic theology views it as a disordering of the faculties of reason, passions, and physical needs and desires. For Protestants, the corruption with which human beings are born through original sin is of a different kind and far more extensive and intensive: a devastation rather than a disordering. This leads us to the next difference between the Catholic and Protestant understandings of sin.

This third difference flows from the position, noted above, that there is a distinction between creation in the image of God and creation in the likeness of God. Catholics believe that the fall into sin *destroyed the likeness* of God but only *damaged the image* of God. The divine likeness is destroyed, thus, all human beings through original sin forfeit righteousness before God and are destined for death. Additionally, the divine image is damaged, thus, all human beings through original sin are damaged in terms of their intellectual capacities and injured in terms of their freedom. With this loss of the divine likeness comes the disordering of the faculties of reason, passions, and bodily needs. But Protestants believe that this Catholic understanding of sin fails to account for the total devastation of human nature through original sin.

The Protestant position represented by the Reformers was that human corruption as part of original sin is characterized by total depravity and total inability.[3] As for the first aspect, *total depravity* does not mean that human beings are as sinful as they possibly could be nor that they lack all moral sensitivity and a will to do what is right (at least on a human level). Rather, total depravity has to do with the *extensiveness of original sin*: every aspect of human nature—the mind, will, feelings, motivations, purposes, and the body—has been infected with sin. There are no elements—the intellect and the will, for example—that escape the devastating corruption of sin. As for the second aspect, *total inability* does not mean that human beings are as evil as they possibly could be nor that they are incapable of moral decisions and actions, including doing good (at least on a human level). Rather, total inability has to do with the *intensiveness of original sin*: people are incapable of reorienting their basic disposition from self-centeredness to God-centeredness. The devastation of sin is such that they are incapable of desiring salvation, taking the initial steps toward God, cooperating with grace, or doing anything that fundamentally pleases God so as to prompt him to be favorable toward them.

When the Catholic and Protestant views of sin and its consequences are compared, the Protestant position clearly views sin and its consequences as more devastating and debilitating. Two examples of this stand out to us. First, Catholics do not believe that original sin includes *concupiscence*, or the inclination to sin. Concupiscence involves the pleasures of the senses, coveting earthly things, and self-assertion. Catholics believe that because of original sin, people have a tendency that lures them toward sin. If they give in to that enticement, they end up committing actual sin. However, this inclination is not sin itself. Protestants disagree: concupiscence, or the tendency to sin, is part of original sin. It brings guilt before God and incurs his wrath. Moreover, concupiscence is insurmountable for sinful people. God's grace alone can conquer it.

Second, Catholics believe that nature (e.g., water, oil, bread, wine, people) is capable of receiving, cooperating with, and transmitting the grace of God. This nature-grace interdependence depends on the view that sin has not utterly devastated nature, leaving it capable of serving as a channel for divine grace. Though nature is tainted by original sin, it retains a capacity to receive, cooperate with, and transmit grace. Yes, Catholics take sin and its consequences seriously, but Protestants believe that sin has a far more devastating impact. Thus, nature can only be viewed as *fallen* nature. As such, it does not possess a capacity to receive and transmit grace.

Biblical evidence of the devastating character of sin abounds: (1) The earth is cursed because of Adam's sin (Gen. 3:17–19; Rom. 8:20–22). (2) Adam and Eve were banished from the Garden of Eden (Gen. 3:24) so as to live in a wasteland—a devastated nature—of their own making. (3) The Word of God came to the world he created—indeed, to his own people—and was rejected. Our only hope is the new birth: not a modification of already existing human nature, but a re-creation solely by grace (John 1:1–13). (4) Even the new heaven and the new earth underscores the theme of re-creation through grace, as the now existing realm of nature is completely renewed through fiery destruction rather than renovation from within (2 Pet. 3:7, 10; Rev. 21:1).

This difference in our view of sin and its consequences sets the stage for a corresponding difference in our view of salvation. For Catholics, salvation is by God's grace that, infused into human nature, enables people to work to merit eternal life. For Protestants, salvation is solely by God's grace that, not finding human nature receptive to it, is imputed as the righteousness of Christ to people's account. We'll have more to say on this topic later.

What is sin and its consequences? Catholics respond, "both (1) original sin, which destroys righteousness and brings death and damages human reason and freedom, and (2) actual sin, which is a violation of God's law and which is of two types (mortal and venial), with serious consequences." Protestants reply, "both (1) original sin, consisting of total depravity and total inability, and (2) actual sin, which is any violation of God's law, with devastating, insurmountable consequences."

WHAT IS THE ROLE OF MARY?

It may come as a surprise that Catholics and Protestants share some common ideas in their understanding of Mary. They both agree with the historical position of the church that Mary is *theotokos*, literally, "the bearer of God" or, better, "the one who bears the one who is God."[4] That is, Jesus of Nazareth, the one who was conceived in Mary's womb and to whom she gave birth, is fully God. This historical confession acknowledges with gratitude the unique role Mary played in the incarnation of the Son of God.[5] Catholics and Protestants are in further accord in appreciating Mary's outstanding model of faith and obedience. When informed by the angel that she, though a virgin, would bear the Son of God in her womb, Mary responded, "Behold, I am the servant of the Lord; let it be to me according to your word" (Luke 1:38). All Christians should desire to offer such "obedience of faith" to the Word of God! Protestants and Catholics are also united in calling Mary "blessed" (Luke 1:48) because God worked mightily in and through her for the sake of all people to fulfill his promise of salvation (Luke 1:46–55).

These three commonalities are all related to Mary's role in the incarnation of Christ. Yet here is where the differences begin as well. Catholics maintain that God "willed that the Incarnation should be preceded by assent on the part of the predestined mother, so that just as a woman [Eve] had a share in the coming of death, so also should a woman [Mary] contribute to the coming of life"

(CCC 488). Many Protestants would agree that Mary's role in the incarnation was eternally ordained, but this is not unusual: God works all things according to the council of his will (Eph. 1:11).[6] However, Protestants do not agree with the parallelism that Catholics draw between Mary and Eve, such that Mary's obedience in giving life to her son reverses Eve's disobedience in introducing death to humanity. Scripture does make a parallel between Jesus as the second Adam and the first Adam (Rom. 5:12–21), but it makes no such correspondence between Mary and Eve.

Catholics expand on the obedience of Mary and hold that in order for Mary to be obedient to the angel's announcement, she had to be well prepared. Accordingly, they appeal to a key declaration from Catholic Tradition: "The most Blessed Virgin Mary was, from the first moment of her conception, by a singular grace and privilege of almighty God and by virtue of the merits of Jesus Christ, Savior of the human race, preserved immune from all stain of original sin."[7] This is the doctrine of the immaculate conception of Mary. Not only at the outset but throughout her whole life, "Mary remained free of every personal sin" (CCC 493). Thus, when Gabriel brought the announcement to her, Mary responded rightly: "Espousing the divine will for salvation wholeheartedly, without a single sin to restrain her, she gave herself entirely to the person and to the work of her Son" (CCC 494). Protestants underscore how the immaculate conception and complete sinlessness of Mary contradict Scripture, which affirms that "all have sinned and fall short of the glory of God" (Rom. 3:23). This sin includes both actual sin and original sin, doctrines that are both affirmed by Catholics. Protestants bristle when such clear and pervasive teachings of Scripture are trumped by Tradition.

For Catholics, the key indicator of Mary's sinlessness was her perpetual virginity. Catholics believe that Mary was a virgin when the Holy Spirit overshadowed her to bring about the conception of Jesus Christ. Protestants agree on this point because the virginal conception is explicitly affirmed in Matthew 1:18–25 and Luke 1:26–38. Mary was a virgin when she conceived Jesus, and she did not engage in sexual intercourse with Joseph the entire time of her pregnancy. Yet Catholics go beyond this and believe that Mary *remained a virgin* during childbirth: her hymen was not ruptured in the birthing process. Moreover, they believe that Mary remained a virgin for the rest of her life. They call her *"Aeiparthenos,* the 'Ever-virgin'" (CCC 499). Mary's perpetual virginity is "the sign of her faith 'unadulterated by any doubt'" (CCC 506) and of her sinless life.

Protestants disagree that Mary's physical integrity was preserved during the birth process. Scripture gives no indication of a virginity-maintaining miracle at Jesus' birth, instead describing it as a very normal event: "She gave birth to her firstborn son" (Luke 2:7). Protestants also disagree with Mary's perpetual virginity because it contradicts Scripture. Referring to Joseph, Matthew narrates, "He took his wife, but knew her not until she had given birth to a son" (Matt. 1:24–25). The phrase "until she had given birth" indicates that after Jesus' birth, Joseph engaged in normal sexual intercourse with his wife. Luke's description of Jesus as Mary's "firstborn son" (Luke 2:7) also implies that Jesus had brothers and sisters, as Scripture confirms.[8]

Catholics also acknowledge a special role for Mary in the Church. They emphasize her union with Christ throughout his life, but especially as he suffered on the cross: "There she stood, in keeping with the divine plan, enduring with her only begotten Son the intensity of his suffering, joining herself with his sacrifice in her mother's heart, and lovingly consenting to the immolation [sacrificial offering] of this victim, born of her" (CCC 964). According to

Catholic teaching, Mary somehow participates in the sufferings of her son. Indeed, in one of his last acts, they attest that he gives his mother to be the mother of all Christians (John 19:26–27). After Christ's ascension, Mary was with the apostles and others in the upper room (Acts 1:13–14). In this role, she "aided the beginnings of the Church by her prayers . . . imploring the gift of the Spirit, who had already overshadowed her in the Annunciation" (CCC 965). For Catholics, Mary is the model of faith, obedience, love, and hope for the Church, of which she is the mother. Protestants disagree with any notion of Mary's co-suffering with her Son, and they consider the idea of Mary's role as the mother and co-initiator of the church to be based on misunderstandings of Scripture.[9]

Because they believe that Mary was conceived without sin, lived her entire life without sin, and was united with her son's sufferings, Catholics appeal to another key declaration from Catholic Tradition: "The Immaculate Virgin, preserved free from all stain of original sin, when the course of her earthly life was finished, was taken up body and soul into heavenly glory, and exalted by the Lord as Queen over all things."[10] This is the doctrine of the bodily assumption of Mary, and it means that she alone has participated in her son's resurrection and is thus the only believer in heaven with a glorified body. As already noted, Protestants disagree with Mary's immaculate conception and sinlessness because these concepts lack biblical support. Catholics appeal to these ideas and not to Scripture in their support of Mary's bodily assumption, and because these ideas are without biblical support, Protestants hold that there is no reason to believe that Mary's body was not laid in a tomb and underwent decay, as happens to all people after death. Protestants also disagree with this doctrine because they believe that heaven is *not* a place for embodied human beings. Until Christ returns, Christians are present as disembodied people in heaven, awaiting their resurrection bodies (2 Cor. 5:1–9). Only at his second coming will Christian believers be re-embodied for their future life with Christ (1 Cor. 15:42–44, 49).

Because they hold these beliefs about Mary, Catholics invoke her "under the titles of Advocate, Helper, Benefactress, and Mediatrix" (CCC 969). They are also devoted to her in a special way. This is not the devotion of *latria*: "worship" that belongs to God alone. Neither is it mere *dulia*: "veneration" that is given to all the saints. Rather, Catholics call this devotion *hyperdulia*: "super-veneration" that is reserved for Mary. Marian devotion includes praying for her to intercede for the faithful and aid them through her gracious intervention. Catholics deny that using exalted titles and having an exalted role for Mary detract from or minimize Christ's unique role as the "one mediator between God and men" (1 Tim. 2:5). Protestants believe that these special roles and titles for Mary undermine the sufficiency of Christ.

What is the role of Mary? Catholics respond, "the sinless, ever-Virgin, second Eve who plays an essential role in the incarnation of Christ and is the mother of the Church as Advocate, Helper, Benefactress, and Mediatrix." Protestants reply, "the unique woman through whom the Son of God became incarnate, who is called 'blessed' for God's work in and through her, and whose obedience of faith is exemplary."

CHAPTER 5

Key Differences between Protestants and Catholics (Part 3)

Church and Sacraments

WHAT IS THE CHURCH?

Nowhere is the divide between the two groups more clearly seen than in the Catholic Church's claim that "the sole Church of Christ . . . subsists in . . . the Catholic Church, which is governed by the successor of Peter and by the bishops in communion with him" (CCC 816). While the Catholic Church considers Protestants to be "Christians" and applauds their devotion to Scripture, grace, prayer, and more, it denies that their assemblies are real churches. Instead, Protestant congregations are called "ecclesial communities".[1] Additionally, while affirming that Protestants can and do experience salvation, the Catholic Church claims that their salvation actually flows from the "fullness of grace and truth that Christ has entrusted to the Catholic Church" (CCC 819). Clearly, Protestants disagree with Catholic teaching on this point.

The Catholic understanding of the church is rooted in two key principles: the nature-grace interdependence, and the Christ-Church interconnection. The first principle leads Catholics to believe that nature is capable of receiving, cooperating with, and transmitting grace when natural elements are consecrated by the Catholic Church. To put this in concrete terms, think of "natural" things like water, oil, bread, and wine. Then, to understand the realm of grace, think of the sacraments of Baptism, Confirmation, and the Eucharist. Catholics believe that through the power of God, nature *conveys* grace, and grace must be *communicated* through nature. Grace restores and perfects nature. This is why Catholics believe that the sacraments are necessary for salvation: they are the means by which grace is infused into people. This grace then operates to restore our fallen nature, enabling us to engage in good works so as to merit eternal life. Baptism, conferring grace through consecrated water, begins this process. It cleanses people of original and actual sins and gives them a new birth. Confirmation, bestowing grace through consecrated oil, continues this process. It conveys the fullness of the Holy Spirit. The Eucharist, giving grace—indeed, re-presenting Christ's sacrifice—through consecrated bread and wine, furthers the process. It augments our union with Christ and separates us from sin. Through the grace infused into people by means of the sacraments, Catholics believe that we experience the transformation of our nature so we can merit eternal life. Nature conveys grace, and grace elevates nature.

Catholics believe that some kind of mediation is needed between the realm of nature and the realm of grace, and this mediation is one reason why we need the Catholic Church. The Church mediates God's grace to nature, and grace needs nature because it must be concretely mediated. It is the Catholic Church's purpose and role to mediate this grace as it consecrates the elements from the realm of nature, administering the sacraments in the realm of grace. The Catholic Church serves as a mediator between these two realms.

A second principle is also essential to the Catholic understanding of the church. The Christ-Church interconnection means that the whole Christ—both his divine nature and his human nature, as well as his body—is present in the Catholic Church. Indeed, Catholics view the Church as an extension of the incarnation. The Son of God became incarnate as Jesus Christ, who mediated grace to nature to bring salvation. In the same way, the Catholic Church, as the prolongation of the incarnation, mediates grace to nature to bring salvation. As the continuation of Christ's incarnation, the Church acts in the person of Christ, thereby mediating between God and fallen people. This mediation is especially visible in the Catholic hierarchy (CCC 875). The Church's leadership—the pope, cardinals, bishops, priests—mediates grace, and the laity—the Catholic faithful—receive grace. It is important to note here that the hierarchy of the Church has more than a mere administrative function. On the contrary, the hierarchy of the Catholic Church is necessary for its very existence as the Church. Through the sacrament of Holy Orders, these consecrated men from the realm of nature become conveyors of grace as they consecrate the sacraments, now in the realm of grace, and administer them to the laity.

The importance of this hierarchy is underscored by the papacy, the office of the pope. Catholics believe that the pope is the Vicar—the concrete, visible representative—of Christ. He is the successor of Peter, wielding the apostolic "keys of the kingdom" (Matt. 16:19). The pope opens the treasury of Christ and the saints and distributes indulgences, or "the remission of the temporal punishment due for their [lay people's] sins" (CCC 1478). He is the pastor of the entire Church, possessing "full, supreme, and universal power over the whole Church, a power which he can always exercise unhindered" (CCC 882). He is the head of the Magisterium, holding the ultimate responsibility for divine revelation by maintaining Tradition and interpreting Scripture. Indeed, the Church claims papal infallibility:

When the Roman Pontiff [the pope] speaks EX CATHEDRA, that is, when, in the exercise of his office as shepherd and teacher of all Christians, in virtue of his supreme apostolic authority, he defines a doctrine concerning faith or morals to be held by the whole Church, he possesses, by the divine assistance promised to him in blessed Peter, that infallibility which the divine Redeemer willed his Church to enjoy in defining doctrine concerning faith or morals. Therefore, such definitions of the Roman Pontiff are of themselves, and not by the consent of the Church, irreformable.[2]

In summary, these two key principles are at the heart of the Catholic understanding of the church: the nature-grace interdependence, and the Christ-Church interconnection. And because of these principles, the Catholic Church claims that "the sole Church of Christ . . . subsists in . . . the Catholic Church" (CCC 816) with the pope and the hierarchy leading it, with particular emphasis on the sacraments mediating grace through nature. Thus, the Church is "necessary for salvation" because "Christ himself explicitly asserted the necessity of faith and Baptism, and thereby affirmed at the same time the necessity of the Church" (CCC 846).

Protestants strongly dissent from this Catholic understanding of the nature of the church. They reject the Catholic Church's claim to be the only true church, a belief that relegates Protestant congregations to "ecclesial communities" that fail to offer the fullness of salvation. Their rejection of Protestant churches is because Protestants do not accept the two key principles just laid out. Protestants do not accept the nature-grace interdependence because it does not account for the devastating impact of sin on nature. Sin has rendered us hostile to, not open to, grace. And Catholic doctrine misunderstands grace to be something that is infused into people, especially through the sacraments, rather than imputed to people from outside of them through a declaration of justification.

Protestants hold that the Christ-Church interconnection is wrong as well: it misinterprets the biblical metaphor of the church as the body of Christ, nearly collapsing the distinction between the two so that Christ and the church become essentially one in reality. Rather than becoming the *same* reality, the metaphor of Christ as head and the church as his body portrays *an intimate relationship of unity* between the two. Moreover, the idea that the incarnation is ongoing and that the Catholic Church is the continuation of Christ's incarnation is contrary to Scripture, which underscores the uniqueness of the incarnation in the person of Jesus. Furthermore, the Christ-Church interconnection contradicts the fact that Christ has ascended into heaven, intercedes at the right hand of God for his people, and is waiting to return to earth. It is not true to say that Christ is here on earth. In truth, he is *not here*, in the church, in the totality of his person. Protestants point instead to the Holy Spirit as "another Helper" (John 14:16) who takes the place of Christ and continues his work among his people.

The Catholic emphasis on the pope, the Catholic hierarchy, apostolic succession, papal infallibility, indulgences and the like is also firmly rejected by Protestants, who find no biblical warrant for such developments and institutions. But instead of simply criticizing the Catholic understanding of the church, Protestants offer their own construction based on the Scriptures. As Protestants broke away from the Catholic Church, they distinguished them-selves from what they considered to be a false Church, and they emphasized the marks of the true church. These marks include the preaching of the Word of God, the administration of the sacraments, and (for some) the exercise of church discipline.[3] According to the Lutheran Augsburg Confession, "The church is the congregation of the saints in which the gospel is rightly taught and the sacraments rightly administered. And unto the true unity of the church, it is sufficient to agree concerning the doctrine of the gospel and the administration of the sacraments."[4] For John Calvin, "Wherever we see the Word of God purely preached and heard, and the sacraments administered according to Christ's institution, there, it is not to be doubted, a church of God exists."[5] The Belgic Confession adds a third mark: "it practices church discipline for correcting faults."[6]

These marks served as a broad guide as various Protestant groups developed different expressions of the true church. Today, diverse Protestant denominations and churches differ among themselves as to church government. Some are ruled by bishops (episcopalianism), others by local elders also who exercise authority in governing structures above the local church level (presbyterianism). Still others locate authority in the church members (congregationalism). Moreover, Protestant denominations and churches differ among themselves in the practice of worship. Some services are highly liturgical in nature, following a classically structured pattern that includes a call to worship, singing, public confession of sin and the promise of absolution, reading of Scripture, prayer, preaching, baptism, the Lord's Supper, and benediction. Other services are slightly liturgical, following a framework that varies significantly from week to week. Still others are characterized by spontaneity, rejecting liturgy as ritualistic, deadening the movement of God's Spirit among the people.

Furthermore, Protestant denominations and churches differ among themselves as to their priority in ministry. Some insist that the church exists primarily to bring glory to God and thus focus on the ministry of worship. Some contend that the church exists primarily to reach unbelievers with the gospel and thus concentrate on ministries of evangelism and mission. Others maintain that the church exists primarily to further the growth of believers and thus highlight ministries of discipleship and education. Still others aver that the church exists primarily to advance the kingdom of God in the world and thus highlight ministries of social engagement and justice. Protestant denominations and churches also differ among themselves as to the sacraments, a topic we'll explore further in the next section.

This dizzying array of Protestant differences can be confusing for Protestants and Catholics alike, not to mention outsiders looking at all of this. What must not be lost in this overview is the unity that Protestants broadly have in emphasizing the need for the Word of God to be preached—the worded gospel—and the Word of God to be celebrated—the enacted gospel—in baptism and the Lord's Supper. All Protestant groups descended from the Reformation hold to the preaching of the word and the celebration of these two sacraments.

And so, we ask, "What is the church?" Catholics respond, "the Roman Catholic Church, which is the extension of the incarnation of Jesus Christ and the mediator of grace to nature, especially through its hierarchy." Protestants reply, "the assembly of Christians in which the gospel is communicated and embraced, and baptism and the Lord's Supper are celebrated (and, according to some varieties, church discipline is administered)."

WHAT ARE THE SACRAMENTS?

As noted above, at the heart of the life and purpose of the Christian community are the sacraments. This statement is certainly true for the Catholic Church and for many Protestant churches today, though some Protestant churches refer to these rites as ordinances.[7] The very fact that the two traditions use different names for these celebrations exposes a divide between the groups.

Catholics and many Protestants define a *sacrament* as a tangible or visible sign of an intangible or invisible, yet real, grace. Holy Orders, for example, is a sacrament involving a bishop's administration of consecrated oil that confers grace on men called to be priests. Other Protestants avoid the term *sacrament*, substituting the word *ordinance* for it. For them, an ordinance is a rite that is to be observed by the church because Jesus Christ ordained it, and it is celebrated by a tangible sign.

Catholics celebrate seven sacraments: "Baptism, Confirmation or Chrismation, Eucharist, Penance, Anointing of the Sick, Holy Orders, and Matrimony" (CCC 1113). These seven sacraments are of three types: (1) three sacraments of Christian initiation: Baptism, Confirmation, and the Eucharist; (2) two sacraments of healing: Penance and Anointing of the Sick; and (3) two sacraments at the service of communion: Holy Orders and Matrimony. In addition to the grace that they bestow, three of these confer an indelible mark: Baptism, Confirmation, and Holy Orders. Because of their indelible nature, these three sacraments cannot be repeated.

Let's take a closer look at these sacraments. We start with the sacraments of Christian initiation. *Baptism*, which is the gateway sacrament, confers grace through consecrated water. It cleanses people from original sin, causes them to be regenerated, or born again, and incorporates them into the Church. *Confirmation* (or Chrismation) bestows grace through consecrated oil and the laying on of the bishop's hands. It confers the fullness of the Holy Spirit, including his power to be on mission. It also increases baptismal grace and unites people more closely with Christ. The *Eucharist*, which is "the source and summit of the Christian life" (CCC 1324), grants grace through the bread and cup of wine that are transubstantiated, or transformed by divine power, into the body and blood of Jesus Christ. It augments people's union with Christ, separates them from sin, unites them with the Church, and commits the Church to the poor.

The sacraments of healing include Penance and Anointing of the Sick. *Penance* (or *Reconciliation*) bestows grace through prescribed "signs, gestures, and works of penance" (CCC 1430) upon people who have committed mortal sin after their baptism. The three required acts of Penance are (1) *contrition*, or sorrow for sin and resolution to avoid it; (2) *confession of sin*, or acknowledging sin to a priest so he can absolve them of it (such confession should take place at least once a year); and (3) *satisfaction*, or reparation for harm caused to others, which is rendered through concrete acts of restitution, compensation, prayer, works of mercy, and the like as prescribed by the priest. *Anointing of the Sick* confers grace through consecrated oil applied on the sick and dying to heal them or to prepare them for facing death.[8] It strengthens people's faith as they approach death, unites them with Christ's suffering, and completes their first two anointings (Baptism and Confirmation).

Finally, there are the sacraments at the service of communion. *Holy Orders* bestows grace through the laying on the bishops' hands to consecrate men to the priesthood. It "confers a gift of the Holy Spirit that permits the exercise of a 'sacred power' . . . which can come only from Christ himself through his Church" (CCC 1538). Three degrees of Holy Orders are conferred: the episcopal office for bishops, the priesthood for priests, and the diaconate for deacons. The sacrament enables bishops and priests to represent Christ to the Church, especially when they administer the Eucharist. Specifically, Holy Orders guarantees that when bishops and priests celebrate the sacraments, their sin cannot prevent grace from being bestowed on the recipients. And it enables deacons to serve the Church by assisting the bishops and priests. *Matrimony* gives grace that initiates and seals a marital covenant between a husband and wife. They confer this sacrament on each other by expressing their consent to be married before the Church.

Instead of seven sacraments, Protestants celebrate just two: baptism and the Lord's Supper. The reason for just these two rites is that they were specifically ordained by Christ and are accompanied by tangible signs. When Jesus gave his disciples what is commonly called the Great Commission, he ordered the church to "make disciples of all nations, baptizing them in the name of the Father and of the Son and of the Holy Spirit" (Matt. 28:19). In saying this, Christ ordained baptism, and the sign for this sacrament is water. The church should continue to celebrate this rite as Christ has commanded us.

In addition, at his last supper with his disciples, Jesus inaugurated the Lord's Supper: "Now as they were eating, Jesus took bread, and after blessing it broke it and gave it to the disciples, and said, 'Take, eat; this is my body.' And he took a cup, and when he had given thanks he gave it to them, saying, 'Drink of it, all of you, for this is my blood of the covenant, which is poured out for many for the forgiveness of sins'" (Matt. 26:26–29). Christ ordained the Lord's Supper, and the signs for it are bread and the cup of wine. The church should also continue to celebrate this rite when it gathers.

But what of the other five sacraments that Catholics celebrate? Protestants do not consider them to be sacraments because either Christ did not ordain them, or their celebration has no tangible sign, or both. *Confirmation* was not something ordained by Christ and there is no sign for it. Similarly, *Penance* was not ordained by Christ and there is no sign for it. The alleged biblical basis for penance to which Catholics appeal is actually a misunderstanding of Jesus' command "Repent, for the kingdom of God is at hand" (Matt. 4:17). In saying this, Jesus did not institute a threefold sacramental action involving contrition, confession, and satisfaction through restitution, prayer, good works, and the like. Rather, Jesus demanded reorientation of one's whole life characterized by turning from sin and to God. *Anointing of the Sick* meets one of the two criteria—oil is a tangible sign—and though it does have a biblical basis (James 5:13–17), Jesus himself did not ordain it. In this sense, it qualifies as a biblical practice worthy of consideration, but not an ordained sacrament. *Holy Orders* was not something ordained by Christ either. While most Protestants ordain their pastors and commission their deacons, such acts of consecration are not sacraments. And while *Matrimony* is indeed ordained by God (Gen. 1:28; 2:24) and endorsed by Jesus (Matt. 19:1–9), Christ did not institute it. Marriage is a rite for people everywhere to celebrate, not something reserved exclusively for Christians.

What are the sacraments? Catholics respond, "seven visible signs of an invisible grace, specifically Baptism, Confirmation, the Eucharist, Penance, Anointing of the Sick, Holy Orders, and Matrimony." Protestants reply, "baptism and the Lord's Supper, as ordained by Christ and administered using water, bread, and wine."

HOW DO THE SACRAMENTS WORK?

To this point we've talked about two key areas of disagreement about the sacraments: the name for the rites and the number of the rites. Before we conclude our look at the sacraments, we also want to note that Catholics and Protestants part company on two additional differences related to *how* the sacraments work. Specifically, are the sacraments means by which grace is infused into their recipients, and is their validity or effectiveness tied to them working apart from the person administering them (*ex opere operato*)?

Catholics believe that the sacraments are means of grace: they actually bestow God's merciful benefits of which they are signs.

Through the consecrated water, Baptism conveys grace that cleanses the baptized from original sin, regenerates them, and incorporates them into the Catholic Church. The grace that is communicated through the sacraments is infused—instilled or imparted—into their recipients, whose very nature is transformed. By this infusion of grace, Catholics are enabled to cooperate with God to merit eternal life. Again, as we saw earlier, Catholics believe that grace *must* be communicated through these elements of nature. At the heart of Catholic theology is this nature-grace interdependence. Because God's grace *must* be communicated through nature, specifically the sacraments, the seven sacraments are all necessary for salvation.

Catholics also believe that the sacraments are valid or effective *ex opere operato*. This Latin phrase literally means "by the work worked" and refers to the belief that, when the sacraments are administered, they confer grace: "By the virtue of the saving work of Christ, accomplished once for all" (CCC 1128), "Christ himself is at work" (CCC 1127) in the sacraments. Accordingly, they convey God's merciful benefits regardless of the state of the man who administers the sacraments and regardless of the state of those who receive them. For example, when a priest pours consecrated water on the head of an infant in the administration of the sacrament of Baptism, that infant is cleansed of original sin, reborn to new life, and incorporated into the Church. This is the effect of the sacrament regardless of whether the priest is the most saintly man ever or if he is engaged in sinful activities. The sacrament is effective in bestowing grace even though the infant is completely unaware of the grace being conveyed. Of course, Catholics would also say that a greater benefit is received by those who are faithful and obedient than by those who simply engage in ritual (CCC 1128).

This Catholic position is grounded on the conviction that because "it is ultimately Christ who acts and effects salvation through the ordained minister, the unworthiness of the latter does not prevent Christ from acting" (CCC 1584). Indeed, as noted above, Holy Orders guarantee that the sinfulness of those who administer the sacraments cannot prevent grace from being bestowed on the recipients. Moreover, when the sacrament of Baptism is administered, it is Christ himself "who baptizes . . . in order to communicate the grace" that Baptism signifies (CCC 1127). Catholics believe that the recipients' faith, which is an essential component of the sacraments, is not first and foremost their personal faith. Rather, it is the faith of the Catholic Church, which bestows the gift of faith on its people. This is what is ultimately decisive for salvation. Indeed, Catholics confess, "It is the Church that believes first, and so bears, nourishes, and sustains my faith" (CCC 168; cf. CCC 1124). The priority of the Church's faith is most evident in the sacrament of Baptism because the infant who is baptized does not express personal faith, but the Church grants the gift of faith to her. Even an adult who is baptized must answer the question posed to him by the priest—"What do you ask of God's Church?"—with the response: "Faith" (CCC 168). Accordingly, the sacraments lie at the heart of the Catholic Church, who is the mother of the faithful—initiating, fostering, and perfecting their faith.

To summarize, Catholics believe that the sacraments are means by which grace is infused into their recipients, transforming their nature and enabling them to merit eternal life. Moreover, they believe the sacraments are valid or effective *ex opere operato*.

Unsurprisingly, Protestants disagree with both of these Catholic beliefs. We would note that some Protestants do consider the sacraments to be means of grace, believing that the water of baptism and the bread and wine of the Lord's Supper are signs, but not empty signs: they truly convey the divine benefits that they promise. However, even those Protestants who hold to this view do not believe that baptism and the Lord's Supper are the *only* means of grace. For example, they would emphasize the power of the Word of God to redeem, transform lives, and restore broken relationships. Also, Protestants who hold to the sacraments as a means of grace do not maintain that the sacraments work in such a way as to infuse grace into their recipients. Rather, they view the sacraments as promises of God's blessing. For example, when Presbyterians baptize the infant children of church members, they consider this baptism to be a sign of the infants' incorporation into the covenant community of the church. And they count this baptism as a promise that these infants will repent of their sins and trust Christ for salvation sometime in the future. Importantly, Protestants do not believe that the sacraments or ordinances are necessary for salvation.

Other Protestants move a step further away from seeing the sacraments as means of grace, instead seeing these ordinances as concrete reminders of God's benefits for them. They view them as testimonies of the faith and obedience of those who share in them. For example, when Baptists administer the ordinance of baptism to people who hear the gospel, repent of their sins, and trust Christ for salvation, the baptized people publicly confess their faith in Christ as they are immersed in water. Their baptism vividly portrays God's grace toward them in putting to death their old way of life and bestowing upon them a new way of life (Rom. 6:3–4).

As for the validity of the sacraments *ex opere operato*, all Protestants disagree with this Catholic position. Protestants believe that the effectiveness of the sacraments rests on God and his promise to confer his benefits through these rites. Because Christ ordained them, baptism and the Lord's Supper come with divine sanction and authority. But it is not Christ himself who baptizes, and it is not Christ himself, through the change of the bread and wine into his body and blood, who is conveyed through the Lord's Supper (to be discussed soon). Moreover, Scripture tells us what benefits the sacraments actually confer to us. Baptism associates new believers with the God who is Father, Son, and Holy Spirit (Matt. 28:19) and pictures those new Christians' identification with the death and resurrection of Christ (Rom. 6:3–4). Scripture is the ground for these rites, and because they are associated with the Word of God, participation in them requires faith. The sacraments are promises based on God's Word, divine promises to be appropriated by faith. This means that non-Christians are prohibited from participating in the ordinances, and the church's expectation is that those who are baptized and those who take the Lord's Supper will walk in faith that is stirred up by the Word of God and the Spirit of God.

How do the sacraments work? Catholics respond, "as Christ himself works, by effectively infusing grace into their recipients *ex opere operato*, thus being necessary for salvation." Protestants reply, "by promising God's blessings, based on his Word and received by faith, or by rendering testimony to the faith and obedience of those who participate in them."

WHAT IS BAPTISM?

Protestants and Catholics agree that the initiatory rite—the initial celebration—of the Christian religion is baptism. Whether in the case of infants or adults, water in some quantity and in some manner is applied to a person in the name of the triune God. For various reasons—salvation, incorporation into the church, a public witness, and more—baptism is a decisive event that is regularly celebrated in both the Catholic Church and Protestant churches. Yet already the tensions can be keenly felt: Is baptism a sacrament or an ordinance? Is it to be administered to infants (paedobaptism) or adults (credobaptism)? Is the proper mode sprinkling, pouring, or immersion? What are the meanings of baptism? Not only do Catholics and Protestants differ over these issues; Protestants differ among themselves.

Catholics believe that "Holy Baptism is the basis of the whole Christian life, the gateway to life in the Spirit . . . , and the door which gives access to the other sacraments. Through Baptism we are freed from sin and reborn as sons of God; we become members of Christ, are incorporated into the Church and made sharers in her mission" (CCC 1213). Thus, the sacrament of Baptism cleanses people from original sin, regenerates and saves them, and makes them members of Christ and his Church.

Let's look at these one at a time. First, Catholics believe that the sacrament of Baptism removes original sin. Because all people are born in this state of both guilt and corruption, infants must be baptized to be saved from sin: "Born with a fallen human nature and tainted by original sin, children also have need of the new birth in Baptism to be freed from the power of darkness and brought into the realm of the freedom of the children of God" (CCC 1250). In the case of adults, whose plight is magnified by the actual sins they have committed, the sacrament effects total cleansing: "*all sins* are forgiven, original sin and all personal sins, as well as all punishment for sin" (CCC 1263, emphasis in original). Secondly, Baptism *regenerates* and saves, according to Jesus' words: "Truly, truly, I say to you, unless one is born of water and the Spirit, he cannot enter the kingdom of God" (John 3:5). According to Catholic interpretation, being "born of water" refers to the sacrament of Baptism, which is connected to the Spirit's work of granting the new birth (cf. Titus 3:5), a process called *baptismal regeneration*. Because no one can enter God's kingdom apart from such baptism, this sacrament is necessary for salvation. Third, Baptism incorporates people into Christ and his Church, making them participants in its mission.

Baptism also stands in close association with the Word of God. Referring to 1 Peter 1:23, Catholics affirm, "Baptism is a bath of water in which the 'imperishable seed' of the Word of God produces its life-giving effect" (CCC 1228). And with regard to faith, it is first and foundationally the Catholic Church that grants the gift of faith to the baptized infant and to the baptized adult alike. Thus, Catholics see Baptism as a sacrament of faith, undergirded by the Word of God, and one that is necessary for salvation.

As we mentioned earlier, there is broad disagreement among Protestants on the topic of baptism. Generally speaking, we can say that Protestants fall into three camps. Some hold to a version of baptismal regeneration. Lutherans, for example, emphasize baptism as a visible form of the gospel and believe that this Word creates faith in infants who are baptized. As Martin Luther explained, "It is not water . . . that does it, but the Word of God which is with and in the water, and faith, which trusts in the Word of God in the water."[9] Methodists maintain, "Baptism is not only a sign of profession and mark of difference whereby Christians are distinguished from others that are not baptized; but it is also a sign of regeneration or the new birth. The Baptism of young children is to be retained in the Church."[10]

A second camp consists of Protestants who practice infant baptism but do not believe that the sacrament regenerates these babies. Presbyterians, for example, emphasize baptism as the sign and seal of incorporation into the covenant community of the church. The old covenant people of God consisted of Jews and their children, and the sign and seal of covenant participation was circumcision. The new covenant people of God consists of Christians and their children, who are baptized to initiate them into the church community. Such baptism does not save infants who are baptized, but the sacrament is far more than a mere dedication. Baptism as a sacrament is a divine promise of grace that effects repentance and faith in the future as these baptized children hear the gospel and believe in Christ.

A third camp of Protestants disagree with all forms of infant baptism and administer the ordinance only to those who hear the gospel, repent of their sins, and trust Christ for salvation. There are a variety of meanings attached to baptism by those in this camp as well, with different Protestant groups emphasizing one or more of the following meanings. It associates new Christians with the triune God (Matt. 28:19–20). It is a vivid portrayal of identification with the death, burial, and resurrection of Christ (Rom. 6:3–4), cleansing from sin (Acts 22:16), and escape from divine judgment (1 Pet. 3:20–21). It is an act of obedience by which people make a public profession of their faith in Christ and are incorporated into the church (Acts 2:38–47). This camp appeals to the instances in Scripture in which baptism was administered following reception of the gospel and to the pattern of baptizing believers in Christ that continued in the early church. They teach that it was only later in church history that infant baptism was instituted to address the problem of original sin (with particular reference to John 3:5), and that this late development is based on a misunderstanding of Jesus' words about being "born of water and the Spirit."

So where does this array of views leave us? We can say that both Catholics and Protestants agree on the important role of baptism, that it is ordained by Christ himself (Matt. 28:18–20). And we agree that narratives of its practice pepper the pages of Acts and that important theological discussions of baptism are presented in the letters of the New Testament (e.g., Rom. 6:3–4; Gal. 3:26–28). From the very beginning, it is clear that baptism has been the initiatory rite of the Christian religion. Throughout history, baptisms have been marked by celebration ranging from elaborate pageantry to simple ceremonies that are joyful, decisive occasions.

Yet when we push beyond this broad agreement that baptism is important and historically celebrated, we find that the understandings that Catholics and Protestants have regarding baptism are characterized more by difference than by commonality. Catholics believe that when the priest pours water on the head of an infant or immerses an adult, Christ himself, through the act, cleanses from original sin, regenerates, and incorporates the person baptized into Christ and his Church. And while Baptism is closely associated with the Word of God and the faith of the Church, grace is infused into people through the water. This view is grounded on the interdependence of nature and grace: nature is capable of receiving and transmitting grace, which must be transmitted through an element of nature. This sacred power is conferred on Catholic priests by the sacrament of Holy Orders, and it is possible because Christ is totally present in the Catholic Church, because the Church is the extension of the incarnation.

As noted earlier, Protestants reject the validity of the sacrament of Baptism *ex opere operato*, even Protestants who hold to baptismal regeneration. Similarly, they reject the nature-grace interdependence and the idea that Christ himself baptizes people. Another important point of difference will be mentioned here and discussed later: Catholics believe that justification comes about by both faith and Baptism, that Baptism is essential to salvation. Protestants believe that justification is by faith, and faith alone.

So what, then, is baptism? Catholics respond that it is "the gateway sacrament that, through Christ's action in it, effectively removes original sin and initiates salvation *ex opere operato*." Protestants reply that it is "the initiatory rite, based on the Word of God and received by faith, which either regenerates, incorporates into the covenant community, or bears witness to one's faith in the gospel."

WHAT IS THE LORD'S SUPPER?

Similar to baptism, Catholics and Protestants share another sacrament that bears some family resemblance in their celebrations of it, yet the beliefs about the celebration are characterized more by difference than by commonality. Nowhere is the divide more clearly seen than in the Catholic Church's prohibition of Protestants from participating in its sacrament of the Eucharist. Even though both Catholic and Protestant celebrations include bread and wine, the recitation of Jesus' words instituting the Lord's Supper, and the giving of thanks, Catholics and Protestants differ greatly over this sacrament, as do Protestants among themselves.

Catholics believe that the Eucharist is "the source and summit of the Christian life" because the "whole spiritual good of the Church, namely Christ himself" (CCC 1324) is present in it. For Catholics, the Eucharist is a *memorial of Christ* and his work of salvation. Importantly, "it is not just a *subjective* experience—the *memory* of Christ—but an *objective* celebration—the *memorial* of Christ."[11] In addition, the sacrament is an *offering* of bread and wine, to God the Father, by its participants. This offering of elements from nature is consecrated so it will infuse grace into the participants.

Moreover, the Eucharist is the *presence of Christ* himself as the elements of bread and wine become the body and the blood of Christ. This change comes about "by the power of the Holy Spirit and the words of Christ" (CCC 1357). As for the first aspect, the Holy Spirit, the priest celebrating the sacrament engages in the *epiclesis*: "the Church asks the Father to send his Holy Spirit" (CCC 1353) to transform the elements. Then, the priest recites the *institutional narrative*, that is, the words that Christ spoke to institute the Lord's Supper during his last supper. As the Holy Spirit is called down, and the words of Christ are voiced, the bread is changed into the body of Christ and the wine is changed into the blood of Christ.

The term for this change is *transubstantiation*,[12] a phrase derived from Latin: "by the consecration of the bread and wine there takes place a change of the whole substance of the bread into the substance of the body of Christ our Lord and of the whole substance of the wine into the substance of his blood. This change the holy Catholic Church has fittingly and properly called transubstantiation" (CCC 1376).[13] Nothing in the outward characteristics of the elements changes: they still look, smell, feel, and taste like bread and wine. But the substance of the bread becomes Christ's body and the substance of the wine becomes Christ's blood. This change takes place at the moment of consecration and continues for as long as the elements exist. Moreover, the whole Christ—both his divine nature and human nature—is present in each grain of bread and in each drop of wine. Thus, whether the participants receive the bread only or both the bread and the wine, they receive all of Christ.

Catholics also believe that the Eucharist is the *sacrifice of Christ*:

> The sacrifice of Christ and the sacrifice of the Eucharist are one single sacrifice: "The victim is one and the same: the same now offers through the ministry of priests, who then offered himself on the cross; only the manner of offering is different." "In this divine sacrifice which is celebrated in the Mass, the same Christ who offered himself once in a bloody manner on the altar of the cross is contained and is offered in an unbloody manner." (CCC 1367)[14]

Contrary to what many Protestants think, Catholics do not believe that Christ is being *re-sacrificed* each time the sacrament is administered. Rather, his one sacrifice is *re-presented* (made present). The explanation for this re-presentation is that Christ's sacrifice shares in the eternal or atemporal nature of God: God is not limited by time, but is always present. So also the once-and-for-all sacrifice of Christ is not limited to the event that happened two thousand years ago. Rather, it is re-presented when the Eucharist is celebrated. In Catholic teaching, the sacrament encourages ongoing *worship of Christ*, whose presence remains in the consecrated elements stored in the tabernacle, a sacred container located prominently in the sanctuary.

Though Protestantism is a diverse movement and Protestants hold to different understandings of the Lord's Supper, all Protestants disagree with the Catholic view of the Eucharist. There are several reasons for this. Foremost, they understand that the idea of physically eating and drinking the body and blood of Christ is based on a misinterpretation of Jesus' words in his "bread of life" discourse (John 6:22–58), "Whoever feeds on my flesh and drinks my blood has eternal life" (v. 54). Jesus was using a metaphorical expression to vividly underscore the necessity of faith in Christ for eternal life, which was the point of the first half of the discourse (vv. 29, 40, 47). But he was not teaching that bread and wine somehow become his actual flesh and blood.

Second, Protestants reject transubstantiation because it is grounded on the Christ-Church interconnection mentioned earlier. Christ is not and cannot be present here in the totality of his divine and human natures, for he has ascended into heaven, intercedes at the right hand of God for his people, and is waiting to return to earth. It is wrong to teach that the whole Christ is present in the Eucharist. Furthermore, transubstantiation is grounded on the philosophy of Aristotle, not on the teaching of Scripture. Because of this, it cannot be an authoritative doctrine that Christians must always, everywhere believe. In fact, the Catholic Church did not proclaim transubstantiation as an official doctrine until 1215, making it a teaching of relatively late origin. Thomas Aquinas, who developed the philosophical foundation for transubstantiation in the thirteenth century, appealed to God's power to effect this change, yet there is no biblical support for this miracle.

Protestants also critique the notion of the re-presentation of Christ's sacrifice, believing that it too is based on an improper literal interpretation of Jesus' words of institution, "This is my body. . . . This is my blood of the covenant" (Matt. 26:26, 28). Jesus' focus in saying these words is on the bread that he is breaking, an action symbolizing the impending breaking of his body on the cross. And Jesus' focus in speaking of the cup is on the cup "that is poured out" for his people (Luke 22:20), an action symbolizing the impending shedding of his blood on the cross. Jesus' words are actions-as-symbols and should not be taken literally.

While it is true that Martin Luther, the great Reformer who led the Reformation charge against the teachings of the Catholic Church, interpreted Jesus' words literally, he also strongly denounced Catholic transubstantiation as an explanation for Christ's presence. His view, called *sacramental union* or *consubstantiation*, does not hold that the bread and the wine become the body and blood of Christ. Nor does it maintain that Christ's sacrifice is re-presented. Rather, the Lutheran position is that the body and blood of Christ are "in, with, and through" the bread and the wine.

As we look beyond Luther's teachings, a wide variety of Protestants interpret Jesus' words of institution as gospel signs: the bread portraying Christ's (future) broken body, and the wine depicting Christ's (future) shedding of blood. John Calvin and others in the Reformed tradition (Presbyterians and Reformed Baptists, for example) would say that Jesus' words are signs, but they are not empty signs. They are signs that convey the blessings that they portray. Calvin's view is referred to as *spiritual presence*, and it teaches that Christ is not present in the bread and wine through either transubstantiation or consubstantiation, but that these signs render his spiritual presence through the work of the Holy Spirit. For Calvin, the Lord's Supper is a means of grace that conveys to us the fruits of Christ's sacrifice, spiritual nourishment, union with Christ and his people, and the like. The Reformed tradition, following Luther and Calvin, denounces Catholic transubstantiation and the idea of the re-presentation of Christ's sacrifice. Moving even further from the Catholic view are Protestants who follow the tradition of the Reformer Huldrych Zwingli. His position is sometimes called the *memorial view*, and it underscores the importance of Jesus' words, "Do this [eat the bread, drink the cup] in remembrance of me" (Luke 22:19; 1 Cor. 11:23–26). Those who hold to this view or a form of it believe that obedience to Christ through participating in the Lord's Supper brings great spiritual benefit.

So what is the Lord's Supper? Catholics respond by saying that it is "the pinnacle sacrament that is a memorial, offering, re-presentation of Christ's sacrifice, and the presence of Christ through transubstantiation of the bread and wine into the body and blood of Christ." Protestants reply that it is "the continuing rite, based on the Word of God and received by faith, which either presents Christ, portrays Christ's spiritual presence and benefits, or prompts remembrance of Christ's saving sacrifice as proclaimed in the gospel."

CHAPTER 6

Key Differences between Protestants and Catholics (Part 4)

Salvation

WHY ARE PEOPLE ACCEPTED BY GOD?

When an infant is carried to the font for the sacrament of Baptism, a Catholic priest blesses and anoints the child before pouring water over her head "in the name of the Father and of the Son and of the Holy Spirit." The child's white garment symbolizes that she has "put on Christ" (Gal. 3:27), and a candle, lit from the Easter candle, signifies the illumination of the new creation. Through this rite of initiation, she who is baptized is forgiven of sin and born again in the Holy Spirit. This gift, which is unmerited, is called "initial justification" (CCC 2010).

With the process of justification underway through the sacramental system, this baptized person can begin to merit for herself the graces needed to attain eternal life. As already mentioned, Catholics believe this is accomplished by receiving the Eucharist and by living a virtuous life. When she commits a mortal sin—a serious transgression by which she falls away from God and loses saving grace—she must observe the sacrament of Penance. She participates by expressing contrition (genuine sorrow over her sin) and

125

confession (recounting her mortal sins) to a priest. Upon hearing the confession, the priest forgives (pronounces absolution) in the name of Jesus and determines the manner of satisfaction or penance: reparation for sin through such activities as prayer, an offering, works of mercy, service, or self-denial. Through this process, she who has fallen away from salvation experiences restoration to grace (and thus a fresh justification) and thus to friendship with God.

If this Catholic believer successfully reaches the end of her life in a state of grace (that is, she is not guilty of a mortal sin), she will ultimately be saved. However, it is likely the case that she must first spend a period of time in "purgatory," an experience of suffering that involves punishment. Purgatory, as the term suggests, is an experience that "purges" or purifies the soul, conforming her to the holiness of God. When she has passed through this experience, she is finally prepared to enter the presence of the One who abides in unapproachable light.[1] This concludes the process of salvation, having originated in her baptism, having grown throughout her faithful life, and having been finally perfected in the divine presence.

So why are people accepted by God, according to Catholic teaching? Or to put it another way, why are they justified? The answer to that question comes down to the application of Christ's righteousness. For Protestants, people become children of God because Christ's righteousness is attributed to them (reckoned, credited to, or forensically imputed). Catholicism, by contrast, teaches that God ultimately accepts people because Christ's righteousness is poured into them (infused or imparted), thus making them actually righteous. This is a key and fundamental difference, arguably the reason why the Reformation happened and the Protestant Church divided Christendom. As John Calvin noted, "the only point in dispute is, how we are deemed righteous in the sight of God."[2]

As we take a closer look at the question of salvation and our acceptance before God, it is important to recognize that Catholics and Protestants both make some distinctions between justification (one's position before God) and sanctification (the process by which one grows in holiness). To affirm the remission of sin is to make such a differentiation, at least implicitly. In other words, to have one's sins forgiven creates a legal distinction between what one *was* before God (guilty) and the way one *is* before God because of grace (forgiven). The key difference that we wish to point out here is that Catholic theology locates the reason for one's ultimate acceptance not simply in one's *righteous status* (as Protestants do, on account of one's union with Christ), but in the *renovation of one's soul* by the Holy Spirit, that is, in sanctification (in a state of grace). Anthony Lane helpfully summarizes this difference for us: "Justification refers to our status before God; sanctification to our actual state. Justification is about God's attitude to us changing; sanctification is about God changing us. Justification is about how God looks upon us; sanctification about what God does in us. Justification is about Christ for us on the cross; sanctification is about Christ in us by the Spirit."[3]

In keeping with this important distinction, Protestants insist that one is justified not as a result of moral virtue or by performing meritorious works (even with the assistance of divine grace) but rather by believing in the finished work of Christ by faith alone (*sola fide*). This justification excludes our works.

Why are they excluded? Because even in our best attempts at virtuous, meritorious works fall short of God's perfect standard. Instead, faith is the divinely appointed way in which sinners receive forgiveness because it does not rely upon ourselves but looks to the righteousness of another. In Paul's words, "For by grace you have been saved through faith. And this is not your own doing; it is the gift of God, not a result of works, so that no one may boast"

(Eph. 2:8–9). Faith has been compared to an empty vessel or an open hand with which one comes to receive divine favor. It is not the vessel or the hand itself that possesses the power. The power of justification is found in the finished work of Christ, which is appropriated through the instrumental means of faith.[4]

Protestants have consistently maintained that saving faith is more than a mere mental assent to the gospel. Rather, it is an active faith that gives rise to hope and love. The apostle Paul concludes his statement in Ephesians 2:8–9 about the reception of grace through faith by stressing that "we are [God's] workmanship, created in Christ Jesus for good works, which God prepared beforehand, that we should walk in them" (Eph. 2:10). And as Calvin famously expressed it, "It is therefore faith alone that justifies, and yet the faith which justifies is not alone."[5] Protestants believe that we are justified and accepted by God because we trust in the righteousness of Jesus Christ, not in our own righteousness. Yet our justification inevitably bears the fruit of our salvation, leading to good works. We'll take a closer look at this subject, the relationship between faith and works, in the next section.

For now, we summarize by asking the question "Why are people accepted by God?" Catholics respond that "grace infused through the sacraments enables them to do good works and become righteous in God's sight." Protestants reply that it is "because of the finished work of Christ on the cross, the righteousness of which is imputed to the believer, accessed by faith alone."

WHAT ROLE DO GOOD WORKS PLAY IN SALVATION?

Catholics commonly object that Protestants are ambivalent toward works. Yet many Protestants protest by saying that works do indeed play a role in salvation. With disagreements like this, it becomes clear that we need to start by defining what we mean when we say that works play a "role." As we just noted, Protestants are united in agreeing that the ground or basic cause or fundamental reason— however one wishes to say it—of acceptance before God is not our own works. Instead, God attributes the righteousness of Christ to believers through the instrumental means of faith entirely apart from works. The cry of the Reformation was *sola fide*, that faith alone justifies. And yet, we should quickly add that genuine faith does not remain alone.

Here is how Italian Reformer Peter Martyr Vermigli relates faith and works: "We do not say that faith through which we are justified is in our minds without good works, though we do say that faith 'only' is that which takes hold of justification and the remission of sins. The eye cannot be without a head, brain, heart, liver, and other parts of the body, and yet the eye alone apprehends color and light."[6] Faith and works must always go together because they both emerge from the believer's union with Christ. Reformers like John Calvin insisted that faith and works run together in the same way that the heat and light of the sun are together.[7] When the sun shines upon people, they feel its heat and behold its light. The two are inseparable, yet distinct. In a similar manner, faith and works are two inseparable gifts that come from the same source. Or to use a contemporary example, faith and works are as inseparable as two legs on a pair of pants. They are not like a pair of socks, which can get separated (and mysteriously lost) in the dryer; they are part of the same article of clothing.[8]

Protestants will also point out that justification, which is by faith alone, is only one of the mighty acts of God in saving us. God also regenerates, adopts, indwells, unites with Christ, anoints, and continually renews us in the process of sanctification. In sanctification, believers are to yield themselves to God's work and engage actively in reading Scripture, praying, worshiping, serving our neighbors, proclaiming the good news, and doing good works that testify to the reality of Christ's new creation. To be sure, like the tax collector (Luke 18:9–14), we lift our eyes to heaven and exclaim, "God, be merciful to me, a sinner!" Indeed, we recognize that our best deeds are as filthy rags in God's sight (Isaiah 64:6). At the same time, we hear Jesus' words as a call to sacrifice: "Any one of you who does not renounce all that he has cannot be my disciple" (Luke 14:25–33 [33]). Such is the cost of discipleship.

So how does the Protestant position on the relationship of faith and works compare to the Catholic understanding? The central difference between the two stems from different understandings of how merit functions in justification. We start by asking whether merit is possible *prior to* justification. According to both Protestant and Catholic theology, the answer is clearly no (CCC 2010). Catholics and Protestants are agreed in saying that nothing that precedes justification can formally merit the grace of justification. However, after justification, the agreement between the two groups is gone. From the Catholic perspective, after a person has been justified, their works are meritorious and they become the reason why God finally accepts them as faithful. In the words of the *Catechism*, "Moved by the Holy Spirit, we can merit for ourselves and for others all the graces needed to attain eternal life" (CCC 2017). By contrast, Protestants dismiss all notion of merit in relation to works. Any claim to merit obscures divine grace, devalues the cross of Christ, and inevitably promotes human pride.[9] From a Protestant perspective, good works illustrate that we have been justified (as fruit indicates the tree from which it is borne) and may elicit divine rewards,[10] but they do not secure our justification or state of acceptance before God.

At this point, we would be remiss if we failed to point out that contemporary Catholicism highlights the fact that God is to be relied upon for salvation over oneself. Interestingly, some Catholics today will use the words "faith alone" (*sola fide*).[11] But their use of this formula should not be understood as equivalent to the position for which the Reformers contended. This Catholic view of "faith alone" teaches that justification requires "a faith formed by love" in a sacramental framework, beginning with Baptism.[12] As the *Catechism* asserts: "The grace of the Holy Spirit confers upon us the righteousness of God. Uniting us by faith and Baptism to the Passion and Resurrection of Christ, the Spirit makes us sharers in his life" (CCC 2017). For the Catholic Church, justifying faith is "alone" in that it does not rely solely upon one's human resources, but it is nevertheless always embedded in meritorious works in the framework of the Catholic sacraments. This view differs from the Protestant view, which puts good works entirely in the category of sanctification as part of a process that follows and is distinct from justification.

In summary, in asking the question "What role do good works play in salvation?", Catholics respond that "they merit for oneself and for others all the graces needed to attain eternal life." Protestants, on the other hand, reply that "works are the fruit of the Holy Spirit, the necessary evidence of faith in Christ, glorifying God and eliciting his rewards, but they contribute nothing to the basis of one's justification."

IS ONE'S SALVATION SECURE?

Yet another difference between the Catholic and at least some Protestant positions lies in the assurance of our salvation. In other words, how certain can we be that we truly have a saving relationship with God? Catholics deny that we can know if we will remain faithful to the end of our life.[13] It is only with the gracious help of God that a believer can persevere,[14] always with the possibility of falling away from grace.[15] The *Catechism,* which affirms that Catholics "can lose this priceless gift" of faith (CCC 162), explains, "*Mortal sin* destroys charity in the heart of man by a grave violation of God's law; it turns man away from God, who is his ultimate end and his beatitude, by preferring an inferior good to him" (CCC 1855). The Protestant Reformers affirmed instead that assurance of salvation is available to all genuine believers. This assurance is based on the power of the faithful God who elects, justifies, regenerates, adopts, sanctifies, and preserves his people. It is further grounded on the pledges and prayers of the Son of God and the sealing and transformative operation of the Holy Spirit. We should note that this position, common among many of the Reformers at the time of the Reformation, is also contrasted with several other Protestant groups including the Arminian, Wesleyan, and Anabaptist traditions. These traditions are closer to the Catholic view in holding that we cannot maintain certainty that those who are saved will persevere in faith until the end of life.

In the "Assurance of Salvation" section of the *Joint Declaration on the Doctrine of Faith,* written and signed by Catholic and Lutheran leaders in 1999, the signers affirm that the faithful can "rely on the mercy and promises of God" in spite of their weaknesses.[16] The Catholic position initially sounds like a strong statement on assurance, sharing the "concern of the Reformers to ground faith in the objective reality of Christ's promise, to look away from one's own experience, and to trust in Christ's forgiving word alone."[17] But this is counterbalanced with the reminder: "Every person, however, may be concerned about his salvation when he looks upon his own weaknesses and shortcomings."[18] Thus, while the language sounds close to the position held by the Reformers, the substance of the Catholic position has not changed significantly. It is simply conveyed in a way that more clearly appreciates God's saving intention.[19]

The difference between Catholics and Protestants on the subject of assurance may be connected to the deeper differences they have concerning the ground of justification. On the one hand, if one maintains the Protestant conviction that righteousness is forensically imputed—reckoned or attributed apart from works—then it is possible to be sure of one's status as a child of God. The grace that justifies one before God enables one to persevere in faith, and one's ultimate standing before God is not based on meritorious efforts. On the other hand, if one maintains the Catholic position that the righteousness of justification is defined as grace infused into the soul, there will always be a measure of uncertainty concerning one's acceptance. Perseverance in justification will always depend upon one's active cooperation with the internally imparted grace and certainly will remain elusive.

Historically speaking, Catholics have often feared that the (Reformed) Protestant notion of assurance potentially undermines any motivation to live a life of holiness: "Why worry about working out your salvation with fear and trembling if it is a done deal?" Catholic salvation holds that final justification is predicated upon good works, so to them assurance appears a form of presumption that gives way to a license to sin (i.e., cheap grace). Abuses in some Protestant churches have added to this conception.

Yet from a Protestant point of view, the problem with the Catholic position is the failure to provide believers with a sufficient amount of security. Numerous passages of Scripture affirm that assurance is the privilege of believers: "I write these things to you who believe in the name of the Son of God that you may know that you have eternal life" (1 John 5:13). Moreover, Jesus promised: "Truly, truly, I say to you, whoever hears my word and believes him who sent me has eternal life. He does not come into judgment, but has passed from death to life" (John 5:24). According to Scripture, the gift of our salvation includes assurance.

A second reason why Protestants understand assurance of faith differently from Catholics is because of the status of believers before God: "But to all who did receive him [Jesus Christ], who believed in his name, he gave the right to become children of God" (John 1:12). Salvation includes not just our justification but also our adoption. It results in a permanent change of relationship in which enemies are reconciled and in which believers become members of God's family. Of course, this does not mean that believers are free from suffering and discipline. God chastens those whom he loves (Heb. 12:5–11) just as parents must sometimes discipline their children. But loving parents do not disown their children. They remain committed to them despite their children's shortcomings. If this is true of human parents, how much more is it true of the God whose covenant love binds him to his people? Because we are justified and adopted, our salvation is secure and accompanied by assurance.

Finally, it is important to recognize the need to preserve a proper tension between confidence before God (on the basis of Jesus' death and resurrection) and the warnings of Scripture against presumption and sloth. Paul tells Christians to "work out your own salvation with fear and trembling" (Phil. 2:12), and this is an imperative we must take seriously. Paul then follows his command with a reminder of the reason why Christ's followers could ever hope to obey it in the first place: "for it is God who works in you, both to will and to work for his good pleasure" (2:13). So while the Bible provides encouragement that God empowers his children to persevere, giving them assurance of salvation, it simultaneously cautions them to avoid the sin of complacency.

So we ask, "Is the salvation of a believer secure?" Catholics respond by saying that "apart from special revelation, the faithful do not possess a present certainty that they will persevere in faith to the end of life." Recognizing that there are differences between Protestant traditions on this question, we can say that Reformed Protestants counter by saying that "on the basis of Jesus' finished work, genuine believers enjoy security in their salvation."

WHY DO CATHOLICS AND PROTESTANTS DIFFER ON PURGATORY?

Since the time of the Reformation, the doctrine of purgatory has been a point of contention between Catholics and Protestants. Protestants see belief in purgatory as a failure to grasp the sufficiency of Jesus' atonement. Catholics, on the other hand, regard the rejection of purgatory as evidence that Protestants do not sufficiently appreciate divine holiness and the need to grow in that holiness. In view of this ongoing controversy, let's take a closer look at the logic behind the doctrine of purgatory.

According to the *Catholic Catechism*, purgatory is a "state of final purification after death and before entrance into heaven for those who died in God's friendship, but were only imperfectly purified; a final cleansing of human imperfection before one is able to enter the joy of heaven" (CCC 896). There are several building blocks on which the doctrine of purgatory takes shape and comes into clearer focus.

First, the doctrine of purgatory depends on the belief that the dead are judged. The first of these judgments is expected to occur at the moment of death and the second on the last day (called the "particular" and "general" judgments, respectively). The intervening time period entails the chastening process known as purgatory. Unlike the Hebrew *Sheol*—the dark, stagnant abode of the dead—purgatory is a place of activity in which the soul of the dead person is perfected. This judgment is most frequently portrayed with the metaphors of fire or ice.

Second, purgatory is predicated on the notion of individual responsibility and free will. While all people share the guilt of original sin, God executes judgment in purgatory upon sins that people have chosen to commit. These are venial sins, minor acts of disobedience, which offend God's holiness without rising to the level of mortal sins.

Third, the Catholic doctrine of purgatory implies a particular understanding of the relation of the soul and the body. With Scripture, Christians affirm that (1) the soul separates from the body at death (to be later rejoined in the resurrection), and (2) the soul is such that it can be punished. On these points, at least, Protestants will agree.

Fourth, purgatory is an intermediary world in which the suffering of the soul may be shortened by the intercessory prayers of the living. During this time, the souls in purgatory are regarded as belonging to "the Church suffering," a real part of Christ's body over which the Church on earth is thought to exercise (partial) authority.[20]

With these building blocks in place, the core question behind the doctrine of purgatory emerges: How do followers of Christ enter the holy presence of God when they have not yet been made perfect? We need to understand that when Catholics talk about purgatory they are *not* speaking about those who are guilty of having committed unconfessed mortal sins, that is, deliberate, conscious, free transgressions of a moral law that involve a serious matter, resulting in separation from God. These mortal sins destroy divine love and compromise righteousness; thus, they make people guilty before God, robbing them of justification (hence the term *mortal*). Catholics teach that the only way to absolve mortal sin is through the sacrament of Penance, which restores people to grace and life.

A follower of Christ whom the Catholic Church expects to enter purgatory is typically someone who has committed unconfessed venial sins. Venial sins are categorically different from mortal sins in that they don't jeopardize one's state of grace (in Protestant terms, they don't cause the loss of salvation). Nonetheless, they are serious offenses and still need *cleansing* and *satisfaction of temporal punishment*. Note that these two expressions are distinct events. The first, *cleansing*, pertains to sanctification. It asks the question, *How are imperfect people able to enter the presence of the holy God?* The second reference, *temporal punishment*, pertains to satisfaction. It asks, *How are venial sins punished when sinful people fail to do penance in this life?* The answer to both of these questions is purgatory. So the logic of purgatory is specifically concerned with these two issues: making believers actually holy and making satisfaction for unconfessed sins. Catholics believe that it is not enough to have simply been forgiven in the past or to have had righteousness imputed (as Protestants believe). Because entrance into God's holy presence requires the complete sanctification and satisfaction of all sins, cleansing and punishment in purgatory are both essential.

Protestants reject the idea of purgatory because they repudiate many of the building blocks that undergird the doctrine. To begin with, Protestants oppose the formal distinction between venial and mortal sins. They also reject the practice of interceding for the dead, and, most significantly, disagree with the concept that God accepts people on the basis of internal renewal. So for Protestants, purgatory is unnecessary. Instead of looking to the cleansing and satisfaction of one's soul through human purgation as the decisive activity that prepares one for God's heavenly presence, Protestants point to the finished work of Christ and his righteousness attributed to believers by grace through faith alone.

It is precisely because the new creation has been inaugurated in Christ that Christians have the hope of leaving this mortal life and being embraced by the loving arms of the Father, quite apart from purgatory. "He has delivered us from the domain of darkness and transferred us to the kingdom of his beloved Son" (Col. 1:13). Indeed, "there is therefore now no condemnation for those who are in Christ Jesus" (Rom. 8:1). "If anyone is in Christ, he is a new creation. The old has passed away; behold, the new has come" (2 Cor. 5:17). "Our citizenship is in heaven" (Phil. 3:20). "You have been raised with Christ . . . where Christ is, seated at the right hand of God" (Col. 3:1). Accordingly, such people are now in union with Christ, with guilt purged, "hidden" and "clothed" with Christ (Col. 3:3; Gal. 3:27). These are the biblical values that raise questions about the doctrine of purgatory.

In the end, we can ask, "Why do Catholics and Protestants differ on purgatory?" Catholics respond that it is "by means of purgatory [that] the faithful are finally cleansed and made acceptable to God." Protestants reply that "Jesus died on behalf of the church, paying the full penalty for sin so that believers would be reconciled to God."

In summary, we have rehearsed in the last five chapters the commonalities that unite Catholics and Protestants (chapter 2) and the differences that divide the two traditions (chapters 3–6). Both Catholics and Protestants rejoice over the doctrines and practices on which they stand together and lament over those on which they stand apart. Given that the Reformation is unfinished, is there any hope for both Protestants and Catholics? We believe there is: the gospel of Jesus Christ.

CHAPTER 7

The Gospel of Jesus Christ

Hope for Both Protestants and Catholics

Most readers of this book will have neighbors, friends, or loved ones who are either Catholic or Protestant. So the question of the Reformation's contemporary significance hits close to home. On the one hand, if one views the Catholic Church as an illegitimate form of Christianity—a false church that teaches heresy—on account of various doctrinal differences related to authority, the nature of the church, and salvation, one will typically adopt an adversarial posture and avoid constructive engagement. On the other hand, if a person considers the Reformation divisions no longer important and the ongoing differences insignificant, the Reformation becomes nothing more than an interesting historical event seen through the rear view mirror as we motor ahead into the future.

Over and against these polar extremes, we want to urge respect for the Catholic Church as an essential part of the broader, historic Christian tradition. In this way, Catholics differ from the Jehovah's Witnesses and the Church of Latter-Day Saints (Mormons) because Catholicism subscribes to the Apostles', Nicene, and Chalcedonian Creeds, and the Catholic Church champions many orthodox Christian doctrines and practices.

On the basis of this conviction, we suggest taking a position that acknowledges and gives thanks for the real agreement that exists across the Catholic and Protestant divide while honestly noting the areas of profound disagreement on a host of issues pertaining to Christian authority, ecclesiology, and salvation.

As Protestants think about the credibility of the Catholic faith today, two distinct questions will typically arise. First, Protestants who take the doctrinal differences seriously will wonder if it is possible for Catholic people to be born-again believers, and second, they will question whether it is right to consider the institution of the Catholic Church as an orthodox Christian church. With regard to the former question, we believe Protestants would do well to remember that although the Bible teaches that one is justified by believing *with* faith alone (Rom. 4:4; Eph. 2:8–9; Titus 3:5), it does not require that one believe *in* faith alone as a point of doctrine. John Piper makes this point when he quotes theologian John Owen, who wrote, "'Men may be really saved by that grace which *doctrinally they do deny*; and they may be justified by the imputation of that righteousness which *in opinion they deny to be imputed.*' . . . Owen's words are not meant to make us cavalier [careless] about the content of the gospel, but to hold out hope that men's hearts are often better than their heads."[1] According to Owen, there are some Catholics who evidently trust in Jesus alone for salvation, despite the teaching of their Church.

Philip Ryken makes a similar point when he affirms the possibility of conversion among Catholics who respond to the gospel, even when such people remain in the Catholic Church:

> Sometimes we forget that Luther, Calvin, and the rest of the Reformers were born and bred within the Roman church . . . and it was within the Roman church that they came to saving faith in Jesus Christ. To be sure, the pope would not

tolerate their plain teaching of the gospel, so eventually they were thrown out of the church. But God can and does carry out his saving work to this day, even where his gospel is not preached in all its clarity.[2]

So, as Protestants, our answer to the question of whether Catholic people can be rescued by Christ through the gospel is a straightforward "Yes."

However, this raises the second question of whether the institution of the Catholic Church constitutes an orthodox body. This is a more difficult question to answer.[3] Because Catholic dogma assigns infallible authority to the papacy, upholds Tradition with Scripture as authoritative revelation from God to be obeyed and believed, elevates Mary as Mediatrix and Queen of Heaven, claims to have the sole authority to rightly interpret divine revelation, and meshes justification with regeneration and sanctification, these doctrines raise questions about any claim the Catholic Church makes to biblical orthodoxy. More pointedly, the question is whether these errors, and others like them, are so egregious that they push the Catholic Church into a category that is *necessarily* non-Christian. As you might expect, this is a question with which the Protestant Reformers themselves wrestled.

The answer of the Reformers is pretty clear. They commonly identified the papacy as the Antichrist.[4] This conviction about the Church reflected their negative feelings about the bankrupt condition of the Church and their belief that the end was near. However, for all of the strong disagreements that Martin Luther voiced against the Catholic Church, he continued to recognize that the Church has a Christian foundation. Luther acknowledged that under the layers of Catholic tradition, the Church possessed a Scriptural core that could truly generate and nurture faith. In his words, "The Roman Church is holy, because it has God's holy name, the gospel, baptism, etc."[5] Similarly, John Calvin held that, despite serious doctrinal differences with his Catholic opponent Sadoleto, such disagreements did not mean that "Roman Catholics are not also Christians. We indeed, Sadoleto, do not deny that those over which you preside are Churches of Christ."[6]

Over three centuries later, Protestant theologian Charles Hodge wrote to Pope Pius IX declining an invitation to attend Vatican I. After citing the reasons why his attendance would not happen, he concluded:

> Although we cannot return to the fellowship of the Church
> of Rome, we desire to live in love with all men. We love all
> those who love our Lord Jesus Christ in sincerity. We regard
> as Christian brothers all who worship, love, and obey him as
> their God and Savior, and we hope to be united in heaven
> with all who unite with us on earth in saying, "To Christ who
> loved us, and washed us from our sins in his own blood, and
> has made us kings and priests to God and his Father; to him
> be glory and dominion forever and ever. Amen" (Rev. 1:6).[7]

Following the lead set by Luther, Calvin, and Hodge, we want to suggest that a helpful way to understand the relationship between Protestants and Catholics is to think of the division in terms of a divided family. Family members may sharply disagree, argue, and move in vastly different directions, but they continue to share a common heritage. Such family members may not even be on speaking terms with one another. Perhaps regrettable things have been said and done toward one another. With candor and humility these offenses are confessed. And when these crucial conversations happen, it is done between family members. The underlying family relationship enables both parties to speak the truth with love and kindness, building on their common ancestry.

Still, to what extent are Catholics and Protestants family members in the Christian tradition? We know that people will disagree about the answer, and we suggest that readers will have to answer that question for themselves. Maybe we are cousins or stepbrothers instead of siblings. Our differences over Christian authority, the church, and justification are indeed great and should not be minimized. But it is also of great significance that we agree on the Apostles', Nicene, and Chalcedonian Creeds, and other orthodox doctrines and practices. For this reason, we encourage our fellow Protestants to respect the Catholic Church as a part of the Christian tradition, albeit one that contains serious error. However, we should also acknowledge that for all its errors, it is categorically different from cults such as the Mormons and Jehovah's Witnesses, which explicitly repudiate the creeds, the deity of Christ, and other fundamentals of the Christian faith.

While the preceding pages have recognized *the issue of authority* as the fundamental dividing line between Catholics and Protestants, it might be argued instead that our divergent views on *the doctrine of salvation* elicit our deepest and most passionate Reformation convictions, at least from an evangelical point of view. For the rest of this chapter, we want to reflect upon the fundamental difference between Catholics and Protestants on the question of the gospel and draw out some of the implications of our disagreement.

The Council of Trent that concluded in 1563 was a watershed event distinguishing the Protestant and Catholic conceptions of justification. Cardinal Avery Dulles has said that the "theology of justification in Roman Catholic teaching has undergone no dramatic changes since the Council of Trent."[8] This raises the question: has Catholic teaching changed at all on this matter since the Reformation? If yes, have there been changes that were short of dramatic but still significant? The answer is yes and yes. Here are a few examples we think worth recognizing.

For starters, Protestant theologian Anthony Lane reminds us that what the Catholic Church said about justification at the Council of Trent was affirmed "at a time in response to what it then understood the Reformers to be saying."[9] This means that we must listen carefully to contemporary Catholic theology to understand the nuances of its current position, especially as it relates to Protestantism. Perhaps the biggest development in Catholic teaching on salvation in recent years concerns its scope. The early church leader Cyprian (mid-third century) asserted "there is no salvation outside of the church."[10] Historically, this affirmation has been interpreted to mean that the Catholic Church is necessary for salvation and that non-Catholics are without hope. Vatican Council II, however, has recast its interpretation to now indicate that Protestants, sincere Jews and Muslims, and even agnostics and atheists may be saved.[11] Two valuable lessons emerge from understanding this development. First, it tells us that Catholic teaching may evolve into a new form, and second, when it does, it does not necessarily disown its past but rather reinterprets it in a new light. While Trent held that all Protestants are lost, Vatican II is clear that this is not the case.

Another significant development of Catholic teaching on salvation concerns the role of merit. As we saw earlier, Catholic doctrine teaches that merits are the rewards earned through God's grace by the Catholic faithful. Divine grace initiates, and the faithful cooperate with it and engage in good works, thus progressing in sanctification, love, and the attainment of eternal life (CCC 2010). Trent firmly rejected the idea that justified people rely upon the imputation of Christ's righteousness in the final judgment. Instead, it argued that justified people lack nothing "to prevent them from being considered to have, by those very works which have been done in God, fully satisfied the divine law . . . and to have truly merited eternal life."[12] In this statement, we see Trent pointing to the "very works" that people have done as having "truly merited eternal life." Yet contemporary Catholic theology qualifies this statement. In its section on merit (CCC 2006–2011), the *Catechism* both restates the traditional teaching from Trent and offers the view of Thérèse of Lisieux (1873–1897), a French nun and Catholic saint who passionately affirmed the need for Christ's righteousness on the day of judgment, the very thing that Trent had refused to accept. In her words to the Savior, she prayed:

> After earth's exile, I hope to go and enjoy you in the fatherland, but I do not want to lay up merits for heaven. I want to work for your love alone. . . . In the evening of this life, I shall appear before you with empty hands, for I do not ask you, Lord, to count my works. All our justice is blemished in your eyes. I wish, then, to be clothed in your own justice and to receive from your love the eternal possession of yourself (CCC 2011).[13]

With this addition, the contemporary Catholic Church underscores what some of its faithful have always known: the sacrifice, love, and righteousness of Christ is the source of their merits before God (CCC 2011).

Perhaps the most surprising emendation to Catholic teaching on salvation has already been mentioned: the affirmation of faith alone (*sola fide*) in the *Joint Declaration*. Responses to the statement often follow one of two extremes. Some use the *JD* to conclude that the Reformation is now finished, or they take the opposite approach and marginalize the statement's significance by casting aspersions upon the document's authority. Yet neither of these responses is warranted. Catholicism's endorsement of faith alone is in fact a real development in Catholic doctrine, even though it falls short of addressing the crucial element of the Protestant position (namely, that we receive forgiveness by faith apart from works). No, it is not equivalent to the view affirmed by the Reformers, and yes, it is definitively linked to the sacraments of the Church.

The discussion of merit leads us back to the fundamental difference between Catholic and Protestant teaching on salvation—the ground or basic reason of our acceptance before God. According to Cardinal Dulles, twentieth-century Catholic theology increasingly recognized the ground of salvation to consist in the (particularly Protestant) notion of grace, that is, divine grace that comes from participation in Christ's righteousness by virtue of personal relationship, as distinguished from an infusion of divine righteousness into one's soul. Accordingly, one's righteousness "always remains a gift; it is a participation in the righteousness of God, given in Christ."[14] While Catholics do not employ the Protestant language of *imputation* to describe the reckoning of Christ's righteousness as the sole reason for one's forgiveness, they are nevertheless keen to underscore the fact that one's righteousness is derived from one's identification with Christ. Dulles concludes, "In that sense the Reformation categories of ['alien righteousness'] and 'imputed righteousness' convey an important truth that Catholics do not wish to ignore."[15]

Despite such significant developments, however, Dulles is correct when he asserts that there have been no *dramatic* changes in Catholic teaching on justification since the Council of Trent. The Catholic Church continues to be nervous about the idea that the foundation of justifying grace consists merely in God's favor, as Protestants believe. To Catholics the Protestant view suggests that people are simply justified in hope, in a mere legal sense. This is why Catholics accuse Protestants of believing in a "legal fiction": that God treats sinful people as justified, that he views them as if they are not sinful but righteous instead even though he knows such is not the case. From Trent to the present day, this concern drives the Catholic insistence that justification is not simply a reckoning of righteousness (*imputation*) but must necessarily involve a process of internal renewal in which the grace and merits of Christ are poured into people's hearts (*infusion*), causing them to be increasingly justified. As the *Catechism* puts it, "Moved by the Holy Spirit, we can merit for ourselves and for others all the graces needed to attain eternal life" (CCC 2027).

This is where we find the rub. And that's an understatement. This is where the sparks fly! Protestants respond to these repeated attempts to focus on internal renewal as an aspect of justification by pointing to the problem of sin, which prohibits people from meriting the smallest measure of divine grace. Because the most impressive displays of human righteousness are unworthy of God's glory and favor, no one can ever achieve, and thus rely upon, human merit. Instead, it is only the perfection of Christ's righteousness that constitutes the ground or ultimate basis of acceptance before God, a righteousness that is accounted to sinners as a gift. Justified persons find themselves clothed in Christ, on the basis of which God embraces them as fully righteous. Unlike Catholic theology, in which the decisive verdict of God's acceptance comes at the end of life following the accumulation of sacramental grace and merits, Protestants emphasize the decisive moment when people believe in the gospel apart from works. They are justified by faith alone, and their perfect standing before God results in new life as children of God, a life that then blossoms with virtuous fruit by the internal renewal of the Holy Spirit through the Word of God.

Growing out of this crucial difference—the question of why God accepts sinners—is the Protestant conviction that the tradition of the Catholic Church presents a deficient gospel. Indeed, Catholics who stand firmly on the Council of Trent without hearing the recent and nuanced contributions of contemporary Catholic thought may actually deny the biblical gospel. But because developments in contemporary theology on justification have moved the conversation forward, there is now a greater amount of space in which to enjoy healthy dialogue and debate on the subject. Such engagement should be cherished as an opportunity to affirm the gospel of the Lord Jesus Christ as our ultimate sufficiency. As Thérèse put it, we appear before Christ with empty hands, not asking God to count our works, but enjoying the divine righteousness in which he has clothed us.[16]

Conclusion:
Is the Reformation Finished?

Yes.

No.

No, but . . .

These three answers seem to be the most natural and common responses to the question that lies at the heart of this book: Is the Reformation finished? Let's see why each of them is correct.

Yes, the Reformation is finished. The last five hundred years have introduced countless changes to Western civilization. While social historians are able to identify common ideological threads that run through these centuries—from medieval Christendom to late modernity—the period in which we now live marches to the beat of a much different drum compared to that of Martin Luther or John Calvin. These intervening years have introduced the secular age—pluralized, democratic, skeptical, subjective, individualistic, materialistic, and nihilistic—an age of unbelief. Such developments have upset the former equilibrium, moving the center of gravity away from traditional allegiances that once pitted Catholics and Protestants against each other.

Think of it this way. In 1517 religious solidarity and national destiny were inextricably linked. In such a world, the notion of religious pluralism was largely unthinkable, and when it eventually found expression, it was frightening. With what church did one choose to identify? Even saying it in this manner is somewhat disingenuous. In reality, there was no pluralistic choice. When Luther wrote his *Appeal to the German Nobility* (1520), for example, he was not suggesting a menu of alternative churches for religious-minded Christians. For Luther, the Protestant cause was a necessary *replacement* of a church that had become compromised. In addition to stirring up deep anguish among rank-and-file Christians, such calls to reform instigated a social and political revolution, one to which the European wars of religion bear witness.

In the context of the Reformation, therefore, words were used to raise concerns, engender emotions, and mobilize individuals for action. In this mix of competing worldviews, rhetorical conventions reflected the severe realities of the day. It was all about conquering (and demeaning) one's opponents. There were no holds barred. Thankfully, however, that day has faded. Instead of quarrelsome polemics, we can now disagree with charity. Instead of drowning or impaling one another across the Catholic/Protestant divide, we may now enjoy a cup of espresso together, pray for one another's families, and cherish each other as friends. So, yes, the Reformation is finished.

And yet, we can also say no, the Reformation is not finished. We say this because of the many basic doctrinal differences that still exist between the Catholic and Protestant traditions. These include views on Scripture and Tradition, justification, the nature and role of the church/Church, the sacraments, the presence of Christ in the Eucharist, Mary and the saints, merits, indulgences, and purgatory. If theological truth is of any importance, we must take these doctrinal differences seriously. Moreover, there is the ongoing problem of multitudes of Catholics who don't appear to have the foggiest idea of what Scripture means by the word "gospel." In the words of Catholic scholar Peter Kreeft:

There are still many who do not know the data, the gospel. Most of my Catholic students at Boston College have never heard it. They do not even know how to get to heaven. When I ask them what they would say to God if they died tonight and God asked them why he should take them into heaven, nine out of ten do not even mention Jesus Christ. Most of them say they have been good or kind or sincere or did their best. So I seriously doubt God will undo the Reformation until he sees to it that Luther's reminder of Paul's gospel has been heard throughout the church.[1]

Given this situation, the Reformation is not and cannot be finished.

Finally, we say no, the Reformation is not complete, but we have made progress in understanding the doctrinal and practical issues that separate us. Common efforts in combatting moral and social decline have brought us closer together. Still, significant theological and organizational divides remain. We recognize our differences and also our commonalities, concluding that while development in mutual awareness and selective collaboration has occurred, key differences still persist. From our Protestant perspective, unless the Catholic Church undergoes radical reform according to Scripture, the Reformation will necessarily continue. An example of such a change would be for the Church to drop its claim that "the sole Church of Christ . . . subsists in . . . the Catholic Church, which is governed by the successor of Peter and by the bishops in communion with him" (CCC 816); thus, it possesses "the fullness of salvation" (CCC 830) upon which all other churches must draw.

On the other side, we would assume that from a Catholic perspective, unless Protestant churches "return home" to Mother Church, the Reformation will never be finished, a move that would require Protestants to submit to papal authority. While we appreciate the growth in understanding between the two groups, and we applaud co-belligerent efforts in addressing concerns within the broader society, Protestants and Catholics are correct when they say that the Reformation is not yet finished.

So how should Protestants who identify with the legacy of the Reformation relate to Catholics around the gospel? In one word, *intentionally*. Precisely because of who we are in Christ—people whose identities are grounded in the crucified and risen Savior—we seek to embody and proclaim the good news. But being intentional doesn't mean we are adversarial or crotchety. In our engagement with Catholic friends and loved ones, we wish to convey the fragrance of Christ—peaceable, gentle, open to reason, full of mercy and good fruits, impartial, sincere, full of grace and truth.

Is the Reformation finished? No, but . . . is our answer.

Now it's your turn. As you think about what we've presented in this book, what is your answer? And more importantly, what are you going to do about it? Whether you are Protestant or Catholic or something else, we urge you to embrace the gospel of Jesus Christ "to be redeemed from fire by fire." Jesus is the sole hope of both Protestants and Catholics—indeed, he is "the only hope" of the world.[2]

Notes

Introduction: What Happened 500 Years Ago?

1. John Wycliffe (c. 1330–1384) was critical of the papacy, the
   Church as the mediator of salvation, transubstantiation, and
   other doctrines and practices. He affirmed the supreme authority
   of Scripture and translated much of the New Testament into
   English. He influenced Jan Hus (c. 1372–1415), who attacked
   the corruption of the Catholic clergy, transubstantiation, and
   heretical popes. In 1415 at the Council of Constance, the
   Church burned Hus at the stake for his views.

2. Martin Luther's initial concern in 1517, when he nailed his *Theses*
   to the bulletin board of the church in Wittenberg (Germany),
   was the Catholic Church's abusive sale of indulgences
   (certificates that claimed to remit temporal punishment for sin).
   However, he soon came to question the Church's exercise of
   divine authority. This was the primary issue at his "stand" before
   the Holy Roman Emperor, Charles V, in 1521. Luther's point
   was clear: Scripture must have the final word over any other
   source of authority, including tradition and church councils. At
   the conclusion of his defense, Luther proclaimed, "Here I stand;
   I can do no other. God help me." It is not surprising that Pope
   Leo X issued an edict of condemnation against Luther, *Exsurge
   Domine* ("Arise, O Lord"), which castigated Luther's teaching as
   a "poisonous virus" (1520).

3. Philip Melanchthon was Luther's protégé in Wittenberg.

Heinrich Bullinger succeeded Huldrych Zwingli as the leader in the church in Zurich. John Calvin fled France for Switzerland where he led the church in Geneva and wrote series of important works, such as his *Institutes of the Christian Religion*. Peter Martyr Vermigli was a prominent Reformed theologian who left his native Italy as the Inquisition was getting underway to teach a generation of Protestants at Strasbourg, Oxford, and Zurich. Thomas Cranmer, the Archbishop of Canterbury in England, laid the groundwork for Anglicanism in numerous ways, including his production of the *Book of Common Prayer*.

4. Juan de Valdés was a Catholic reformer who led an influential circle of evangelicals in Naples. Cardinal Giacomo Sadoleto, Bishop of Carpentras near Avignon (France), worked closely with Pope Paul III, attempting to promote renewal. Cardinal Giovanni Morone was the Bishop of Modena (Italy). Reginald Pole was an English Cardinal who led the renewal movement known as the *Spirituali*. He was also the last Roman Catholic Archbishop of Canterbury. Tommaso Badia was a Dominican Cardinal who helped to establish the Society of Jesus.

5. Thomas Bokenkotter, *A Concise History of the Catholic Church* (New York: Doubleday, 2004), 250–251.

6. Eva-Marie Jung, "On the Nature of Evangelism in Sixteenth-Century Italy," *Journal of the History of Ideas* 14 (1953): 511–527 (513). J. D. Mansi, *Sacrorum Conciliorum Nova Amplissima Collectio*, 32.669.

7. This specific phrase is a product of later systematic theologians, coined in the Netherlands in the seventeenth century and not the sixteenth century.

8. Martin Luther originally considered penance to be a third sacrament. Martin Luther, *On the Babylonian Captivity of the Church*, in *LW*, 36:243–244.

9. The Pew Forum on Religion and Public Life, "Faith in Flux: Changes in Religious Affiliation in the U.S. (Executive

Summary, April 2009, rev. 2011)," *Pew Research Center*, http://
pewforum.org/Faith-in-Flux.aspx.

10. Roland Bainton, *Women of the Reformation in Germany and Italy*
(Minneapolis, Minn.: Augsburg, 1971), 167.

11. Timothy George, "Nicodemism," in *The Oxford Encyclopedia of
the Reformation*, ed. Hans Hillerbrand, 4 vols. (New York: Oxford
University Press, 1996), 3:144. His biblical reference is John 3:2.

12. Joseph C. McLelland, "Valdés and Vermigli: Spirituality and the
Degrees of Reform," in *Peter Martyr Vermigli and the European
Reformations: Semper Reformanda*, ed. Frank A. James, III
(Leiden: Brill, 2004), 238–250 (248).

13. http://www.pewforum.org/2015/05/12/americas-changing-
religious-landscape/. Accessed on August 2, 2015.

14. Based on an earlier Pew Forum study, updated in February of
2011. http://www.pewforum.org/2009/04/27/faith-in-flux/.
Accessed on August 2, 2015.

15. Timothy George, "Catholics and Evangelicals in the Trenches,"
Christianity Today (May 16, 1994): 16.

16. This was true in the election of 1928, when Al Smith ran for
office, and in 1961 when John F. Kennedy became the president
of the United States.

Chapter 1: How Do the Fundamental Commitments of Catholics and Protestants Differ?

1. For a sampling of such stories, see Robert L. Plummer, gen. ed.,
*Journeys of Faith: Evangelicalism, Eastern Orthodoxy, Catholicism,
and Anglicanism* (Grand Rapids: Zondervan, 2012), especially
chapters 2 and 3.

2. John Henry Newman, *Apologia Pro Vita Sua: Being a History
of His Religious Opinions* (London: Longmans, Green and Co.,
1882), 5. Hereafter abbreviated as *Apologia*.

3. Ian Ker, *John Henry Newman: A Biography* (Oxford: Clarendon, 2009), 92.

4. John Henry Newman, *Autobiographical Writings*, ed. Henry Tristram (London: Sheed and Ward, 1956), 78.

5. J. C. Ryle, *Knots Untied: Being Plain Statements on Disputed Points in Religion from the Standpoint of an Evangelical Churchman* (London: National Protestant Church Union, 1898), 3.

6. John Henry Newman, *Letters and Diaries of John Henry Newman*, ed. Charles Stephen Dessain, et al., 32 vols. (London: Thomas Nelson, 1961–77), 4:304.

7. See Gregg R. Allison, *Roman Catholic Theology and Practice: An Evangelical Assessment* (Wheaton, Ill.: Crossway, 2014).

8. Richard John Neuhaus, "The Catholic Difference," in *Evangelicals and Catholics Together: Toward a Common Mission*, ed. Charles Colson and Richard John Neuhaus (Dallas: Word, 1995), 216.

9. Pope Benedict XVI, *Joseph Ratzinger in* Communio, Volume 1: *The Unity of the Church* (Grand Rapids: Eerdmans, 2010), 73–74.

10. Protestants make this case in a variety of ways. For instance, Mark Saucy uses the *munus triplex Christi* (the threefold office of Christ as prophet, priest, and king) to explain how the grounding of sacramental ecclesiology and soteriology is a misappropriation of incarnation theology. See Saucy, "Evangelicals, Catholics, and Orthodox Together: Is the Church the Extension of the Incarnation?" *JETS* 43 (2000): 193–212. In the vein of biblical theology, Leonardo De Chirico's work compares the biblical adverbs *hapax* (a one-time occurrence) and *mallon* (a continuous process) in light of Jesus' ascension to suggest that the Catholic emphasis on Christological continuation confuses redemptive historical time distinctions. See De Chirico, "The Blurring of Time Distinctions in Roman Catholicism," *Themelios* 29 (2004): 40–46. Similar to this is Herman Ridderbos's evaluation of Paul's "head" and "body" metaphors, the discontinuity of which, he argues, militates

against the Catholic position. See Ridderbos, *Paul: An Outline of His Theology*, trans. John Richard De Witt (Grand Rapids: Eerdmans, 1975), 362–93. Kevin Vanhoozer's canonical linguistic approach is also illuminating, particularly as it differentiates the canonical script from the faith community. See Vanhoozer, *The Drama of Doctrine: A Canonical Linguistic Approach to Christian Theology* (Louisville, Ky.: Westminster John Knox, 2005). Gregg Allison argues against the Catholic position by pointing to the ascension and return of Christ. *Roman Catholic Theology and Practice*, 149, 151, 157.

11. Jesus is described as God's Word, for instance, in John's gospel: "In the beginning was the Word, and the Word was with God, and the Word was God" (John 1:1; cf. 1 John 1:1; Rev. 19:13).

12. Through Scripture, God grants new life (John 5:24; 6:63; Rom. 10:8–10; Eph. 1:13; James 1:18; 1 Pet. 1:23–25), reveals his will (Matt. 4:4; 7:21; 1 Tim. 4:6–16; 2 Tim. 2:15; 3:16–17), and rules over his people (John 17:17; 1 Cor. 14:37; Phil. 2:16; 1 Tim. 5:17).

13. Alister McGrath, *Christianity's Dangerous Idea: The Protestant Revolution—A History from the Sixteenth Century to the Twenty-First* (New York: HarperCollins, 2007), 201.

14. The following summary is supported by the *Catechism* (CCC 1997–2011) and representative documents such as The Gospel Coalition Confessional Statement, 7–8.

15. Anthony N. S. Lane, *Justification by Faith in Catholic-Protestant Dialogue: An Evangelical Assessment* (London: T & T Clark, 2002), 124. "Tony" is Professor of Historical Theology at the London School of Theology.

16. *JD*, 41–44.

17. Ibid., 42.

18. Lane, *Justification by Faith*, 223.

19. Paul T. McCain, "A Betrayal of the Gospel: The Joint Declaration on the Doctrine of Justification," *First Things* (March 12, 2010), http://www.firstthings.com/blogs/firstthoughts/2010/03/a

-betrayal-of-the-gospel-the-joint-declaration-on-the-doctrine-of
-justification.

20. Mark A. Noll and Carolyn Nystrom, *Is the Reformation Over?
An Evangelical Assessment of Contemporary Roman Catholicism*
(Grand Rapids: Baker, 2005), 17. The statement "Things are not
the way they used to be" is the title of their first chapter.

21. Ibid., 114.

22. Ibid., 237.

23. Ibid., 251.

Chapter 2: Where Protestants and Catholics Stand Together

1. To "spirate" means to breathe out. Theologically, "spirate"
refers to the eternal act of the Father and Son to grant to the
third person of the Trinity his person-of-the-Spirit. Because of
spiration, the Holy Spirit proceeds from the Father and the Son.

2. According to Jesus' own affirmations in the upper room
discourse (John 14–17), the Father will send the Holy Spirit
in Jesus' name, and the Son will send the Holy Spirit from the
Father. Though his promise refers to the Father and the Son
sending the Holy Spirit on the day of Pentecost to inaugurate
his new covenant ministry, the question is raised: Why do those
two send the Holy Spirit? The Western Church (Catholic and
Protestant) has historically appealed to the eternal procession of
the Holy Spirit from both the Father and the Son to answer the
question. He is the Spirit of God (the Father) and the Spirit of
Christ (the Son), as Paul underscores in Romans 8:9.

3. This section on the divine attributes reflects the definitions
of them as developed in Gregg R. Allison, *The Baker Compact
Dictionary of Theological Terms* (Grand Rapids: Baker, 2016).

4. Protestants typically refer to this as *special revelation*, whereas
Catholics call it *divine revelation*.

5. For a brief discussion of Tradition and tradition, see Gregg R.

Allison, *Historical Theology: An Introduction to Christian Doctrine*
(Grand Rapids: Zondervan, 2011), 23n2.

6. The Protestant hesitancy is due to the fact that appeals to the
analogy of being may blur the Creator-creature distinction, that
is, the infinite difference between God and human beings.

7. *Monophysitism* comes from the Greek word signifying "one
nature": *mono* = one; *phusis* = nature.

8. *Dythelitism* comes from the Greek word signifying "two wills": *di*
= two; *thelēma* = will. *Monothelitism* comes from the Greek word
signifying "one will": *mono* = one; *thelēma* = will.

9. Though this quote comes from the Catholic perspective, a
similar view is expressed by Martin Luther, John Calvin, and
many other Protestants.

10. As before, though this citation represents the Catholic viewpoint,
a similar idea is expressed by Protestants.

11. "Dichotomy" comes from the Greek word signifying "to cut into
two": *dichē* = two; *temnō* = to cut (into parts); thus, one material
aspect and one immaterial aspect. "Trichotomy" comes from the
Greek word signifying "to cut into three": *trichē* = three; *temnō* =
to cut (into parts); thus, one material aspect and two immaterial
aspects, popularly understood as the soul, consisting of the
intellect, emotions, and will; and the spirit, being that element
by which people relate to God.

12. Within both Catholic and Protestant theologies, various
positions on the relationship between God's role and the human
role in the application of salvation can be found. The position
expressed here is the Augustinian and Reformed/Calvinist view.

13. *Millennium* comes from the Latin *mille*, or thousand, and
annum, or year. Thus, the millennium is a thousand years. The
Bible presents the millennium in Revelation 20:1–6.

Chapter 3: Key Differences between Protestants and Catholics (Part 1)

1. This affirmation does not mean that Protestantism ignores or rejects the theological wisdom that it has inherited from the church throughout the ages (a point to be made shortly).

2. Factors that contributed to this development included: (1) exaggerated and indefensible claims for papal authority not only over the Catholic Church but the entire world as well; (2) theoretical debates over which of the two options—the authority of Scripture and the authority of the Church—is supreme; (3) the introduction of the idea of apostolic succession; and (4) the novel claim that, because the Church had determined the canon of Scripture, the Church therefore possesses special revelation that is not found in Scripture. See Gregg R. Allison, *Historical Theology: An Introduction to Christian Doctrine* (Grand Rapids: Zondervan, 2011), especially chapters 4 and 7.

3. In more detail, Protestants gratefully use tradition (not Tradition, as in the Catholic sense), or wisdom from the past, as a servant to help their churches engage in the proper understanding and application of Scripture and the formulation of sound doctrine.

4. This attribute does not mean that people have to possess a written copy of Scripture and be able to read it. Rather, in the case of the majority of people today in whose language Scripture has yet to be translated and/or if those people are illiterate, they only need to be able to understand oral communication. Scripture read and heard is God's necessary Word for them.

5. Augustine, *Letter 82*, in *NPNF*1, 1:348. His reference to a faulty manuscript means that an error had been introduced when the original text of Scripture was copied. His reference to a translator means that the person who had translated the text of Scripture into the Latin Vulgate had done a poor job, not rendering a

proper meaning in the Latin version. (Augustine was not a
scholar in Hebrew and Greek and thus had to rely on a Latin
translation of the Bible.)

6. Cardinal König provided several examples of alleged errors in
the Bible: (1) Mark 2:26, according to which David "entered the
house of God, in the time of Abiathar the high priest, and ate the
bread of the Presence," conflicts with 1 Samuel 21:1–6, which
locates this event during the high priesthood of Ahimelech,
Abiathar's father. (2) Matthew 27:9, according to which the
purchase of a potter's field with Judas's betrayal money "fulfilled
what had been spoken by the prophet Jeremiah," is actually the
fulfillment of the prophecy of Zechariah 11:12–13. (3) The date
assigned to the time of Nebuchadnezzar's siege of Jerusalem by
Daniel 1:1—"in the third year of the reign of Jehoiakim king of
Judah" (607 BC)—conflicts with an extra-biblical chronicle of
King Nebuchadnezzar that places the outset of the siege three
years later in 610 BC.

As for the first alleged error, Mark's expression *"in the
time of* Abiathar the high priest" refers to a general time period
that included the high priesthood of Abiathar's son Ahimelech.
Ahimelech followed his father as high priest after Abiathar was
struck down by Saul (1 Sam. 22:6–23). Concerning the second
alleged error, Matthew actually references a passage in Jeremiah
and alludes to Zechariah 11:12–13. One notes the remarkable
parallels between the incident involving Judas in Matthew 27
and the incident narrated in Jeremiah 19. Both accounts feature
betrayal by the shedding of innocent blood, the renaming of a
locality with an expression denoting violence, a place becoming
a burial ground, a potter, and the involvement of priests and
elders. Matthew alludes to Zechariah 11:12–13 as well because
of its strong parallels to the incident involving Judas. The fusion
of sources—Zechariah and Jeremiah—under one reference—
Jeremiah—is not uncommon in Scripture (e.g., Mark 1:1–3

actually fuses three sources under one reference, Isaiah).
Matthew's notion of "fulfillment," then, was not so much "this
prophecy came about in terms of this fulfillment" as it was "this
tragic situation (the incident involving Judas) stands in stark
parallel to other tragic incidents" (Jer. 19; Zech. 11:12–13).
Regarding the third alleged error, scholars are not convinced of
the accuracy of dating as found in the extra biblical chronicle
of King Nebuchadnezzar. Thus, there are plausible solutions to
Cardinal König's alleged errors in Scripture.

7. Raymond Brown and Thomas Aquinas Collins, in an article
in the *New Jerome Biblical Commentary*, exemplify the non-
inerrantist interpretation: "On inerrancy Vatican II made an
important qualification as our own italics indicate: 'The Books
of Scripture must be acknowledged as teaching firmly, faithfully,
and without error *that truth which God wanted put into the sacred
writings for the sake of our salvation*.' Some have tried to interpret
the italicized phrase to cover everything the human author
expressed; but pre-voting debates show an awareness of errors
in the Bible. Thus, it is proper to take the clause as specifying
Scriptural teaching is truth without error to the extent that it
conforms to the salvific purposes of God." Raymond Brown
and Thomas Aquinas Collins, "Church Pronouncements" in
Raymond Brown, ed., *NJBC* (Englewood Cliffs, N.J.: Prentice
Hall, 1990), 1169.

8. The other authorities cited are Thomas Aquinas, the Council of
Trent, Leo XIII's encyclical *Providentissimus Deus*, and Pius XII's
encyclical *Divino Afflante Spiritus*.

9. Note the slight change at the end: not Ecclesiastes, which both
Catholic and Protestant versions include, but Ecclesiasticus,
which the Catholic version alone includes.

10. This list follows the order of Josephus's canon (*Against Apion*
1.37), but it numbers and names the writings according to the
English Bible. For example, in the Hebrew Bible, Samuel is

one book, but in the English Bible, and thus in the above list, it is 1 Samuel and 2 Samuel. The same approach applies to Judges–Ruth, Kings, Jeremiah–Lamentations, the Twelve Minor Prophets (one book in the Hebrew Bible, twelve books in the English Bible), Ezra–Nehemiah, and Chronicles.

11. The abbreviation LXX, or Seventy, became associated with this translation because of the tradition that seventy translators worked on it in Alexandria, Egypt. Though these men worked separately from one another, their seventy translations turned out to be identical. This tradition is an urban legend with no basis in reality.

12. The apocryphal writings in the Septuagint, while including all those books that would later be included in the Latin Vulgate, contained other writings as well (e.g., 1 Esdras; the Prayer of Manasseh).

13. Jerome, *Preface to the Books of Samuel and Kings*, NPNF2 6:490.

14. Jerome, *Preface to the Books of Proverbs, Ecclesiastes, and the Song of Solomon*, NPNF2 6:492.

15. *Canons and Decrees of the Council of Trent*, 4th session (April 8, 1546), *Decree Concerning the Canonical Scriptures*, in Schaff, 2:80. The text has been rendered clearer.

16. Allison, *Roman Catholic Theology and Practice*, 80.

17. Ibid., 97. Support for this presumption of continued intelligibility includes (1) Deut. 30:11–14: Moses affirms that the instruction that he was giving to the people of Israel is not too difficult for them to understand; (2) Deut. 31:9–13: Moses commands the leaders of the people of Israel to assemble regularly the men, women, children, and foreigners in their midst and to read Scripture to them, so the hearers could understand and obey it; and (3) 1 Cor. 10:1–11: Paul references four Old Testament stories of Jewish sin and divine judgment, with the expectation that the Gentile Christians would understand those narratives and be warned by them.

18. Reasons for the Reformers' rejection of the Catholic interpretive

approach include: (1) It destroys Scripture. (2) It has poor
biblical grounding (e.g., 2 Cor. 3:6 provides no justification for
a multiple meaning approach, as Catholics claim). (3) It lacks
the support of biblical authority, early church leaders, and basic
principles of grammar. (4) It contradicts the simple writing
of the Holy Spirit. And (5) it violates the logic of effective
communication. See Allison, *Historical Theology*, 173–175.

19. Martin Luther, *Answers to the Hyperchristian, Hyperspiritual,
    Hyperlearned Book by Goat Emser in Leipzig*, in *LW*, 39:177.

20. Martin Luther, *Prefaces to the New Testament*, in *LW*, 35:396.

21. To clarify the difference between Protestant typology and
    Catholic allegory: Typology is limited to the intended
    relationship between Old Testament types and their New
    Testament antitypes. This connection is drawn out by the New
    Testament authors. Allegory is meaning that is found in all, or
    almost all, passages of Scripture, so it is not limited by the New
    Testament writers' use of the Old Testament.

Chapter 4: Key Differences between Protestants and Catholics (Part 2)

1. For example, take the second description of human creation in the
   image of God in Genesis 5: "This is the book of the generations
   of Adam. When God created man, he made him *in the likeness of
   God*. Male and female he created them, and he blessed them and
   named them Man when they were created. When Adam had lived
   130 years, he fathered a son *in his own likeness, after his image*, and
   named him Seth" (Gen. 5:1–3; emphasis added). Being made in
   the divine *image* is being made in the divine *likeness*. Being made
   in Adam's *likeness* is being made in Adam's *image*. The two words
   are synonyms for one another. For a broad discussion of such
   linguistic issues, see James Barr, *The Semantics of Biblical Language*
   (Oxford: Oxford University Press, 1961).

2. Chris Rice, "Big Enough," from *Past the Edges* (Sony, 1998).

3. This discussion represents the view of sin from a Reformed perspective. Other Protestant theologies, like Arminianism, are in some ways similar to the Catholic view.

4. Pelikan renders *theotokos* as "the one who gives birth to the one who is God." Jaroslav Pelikan, *Mary through the Centuries* (Cambridge, Mass.: Yale University Press, 1998), 55.

5. The Council of Ephesus (431) affirmed Mary as *theotokos* against the heretical Christology of Nestorius. Only later did the confession become a recognition of the exalted status of Mary.

6. Furthermore, when Catholics emphasize that "after a long period of time of waiting the times are fulfilled in her [Mary] . . . and the new plan of salvation is established" (CCC 489), they deflect the proper emphasis that Scripture places on Jesus: "But *when the fullness of time had come,* God sent forth *his Son,* born of woman, born under the law, to redeem those who were under the law, so that we might receive adoption as sons" (Gal. 4:4–5, emphasis added). The fulfillment of the long period of waiting for God's salvation is the incarnation of the Son and his crucifixion, not the arrival and work of Mary.

7. Pius IX, *Ineffabilis Deus* (December 8, 1854). The encyclical is accessible at: http://www.papalencyclicals.net/Pius09/p9ineff.htm.

8. For Jesus' brothers and sisters, see Matthew 12:46; Mark 3:31; Luke 8:19; 13:55–56; and Acts 1:14.

9. For example, the Catholic interpretation of John 19:26–27 allegorizes the apostle John, who becomes humanity in general and Christians in particular. Thus, as John, representing humanity and the Church, is given to Mary, she becomes the mother of all. The Catholic interpretation also downplays the fact that in the narrative, John takes Mary into *his* home. This act on the part of Jesus should be seen as his kindness to provide for his mother as he is being crucified. It should not be minimized so that Jesus' action becomes a warrant for Mary's

special role. Most importantly, the Catholic interpretation, focusing on Mary's role, downplays the passage's emphasis on Jesus and his death (John 19:28–30).

10. Pius XII, *Munificentissimus Deus* (November 1, 1950); accessible at http://w2.vatican.va/content/pius-xii/en/apost_constitutions/documents/hf_p-xii_apc_19501101_munificentissimus-deus.html.

Chapter 5: Key Differences between Protestants and Catholics (Part 3)

1. As affirmed in the *motu proprio* of Pope Benedict XVI, "Responses to Some Questions Regarding Certain Aspects of the Doctrine of the Church" (July 10, 2007). Accessible at http://www.vatican.va/roman_curia/congregations/cfaith/documents/rc_con_cfaith_doc_20070629_responsa-quaestiones_en.html. Accessed April 18, 2016.

2. Vatican Council I, *Pastor Aeternus* (July 18, 1870).

3. As noted earlier, Protestant theology agrees with Catholic theology regarding the four classical attributes of the church: unity, holiness, catholicity, and apostolicity. Still, the two would define these four characteristics differently. Thus, while agreeing with the attributes of the church, Protestants at the time of the Reformation denied that the Catholic Church properly embodied those attributes because of the political corruption, sexual immorality, spiritual bankruptcy, and the like into which the Church had fallen.

4. *Augsburg Confession*, 7, in Schaff, 3:11–12.

5. John Calvin, *Institutes*, 4.1.9.

6. *Belgic Confession*, 29, in Schaff, 3:383. The *Scottish Confession* also includes this third mark: "ecclesiastical discipline uprightly ministered, as God's word prescribes, whereby vice is repressed, and virtue nourished." *Scottish Confession of Faith*, 18, in Schaff, 3:486.

7. The term *rite* refers to an action that is administered according to some protocol or formal structure. It should not be confused with the idea of *ritual* as an activity in which a person engages without thought and thus as a meaningless duty.

8. This sacrament is ideally preceded by Penance and the Eucharist.

9. Martin Luther, *Small Catechism*, 4.3, in Schaff, 3:86.

10. (Methodist) *Articles of Religion*, 17.

11. Allison, *Roman Catholic Theology and Practice*, 302.

12. Transubstantiation is from *trans*, or change, and *substantia*, or substance (that which makes something what it is).

13. The citation is taken from the *Canons and Decrees of the Council of Trent*, 13th session (October 11, 1551), *Decree Concerning the Most Holy Sacrament of the Eucharist*, 4, in Schaff, 2:130.

14. The citations are taken from the *Canons and Decrees of the Council of Trent*, 22nd session (September 17, 1562), *Decree Concerning the Most Holy Sacrifice of the Mass*, 2, in Schaff, 2:179; cf. Heb. 9:14, 27.

Chapter 6: Key Differences between Protestants and Catholics (Part 4)

1. A primary reason why Protestants reject the doctrine of purgatory is that it denies the sufficiency of Christ's atoning death. According to the writer of Hebrews, "For by one sacrifice [Jesus Christ] has made perfect forever those who are being made holy" (Heb. 10:14 NIV). Indeed, Jesus himself exclaimed from the cross, "It is finished" (John 19:30). From such texts, Protestants assert that it is not purgation *after* the cross, but purgation *of* the cross, that makes us acceptable to God.

2. John Calvin, *Acts of the Council of Trent: with the Antidote 6th Session*, in Henry Beveridge, ed., *Tracts and Treatises of John Calvin*, 3 vols. (Eugene, Ore.: Wipf & Stock, 2002), 3:118.

3. Anthony N. S. Lane. "Ten Theses on Justification and

Sanctification," in Antony Billington, Tony Lane, Max Turner, eds., *Mission and Meaning: Essays Presented to Peter Cotterell* (Carlisle: Paternoster, 1995), 193.

4. John Calvin, *Institutes*, 3.11.7.

5. Calvin, *Acts of the Council of Trent*, 3:152.

6. Vermigli, *Romanos*, 1312 [218]. The text has been rendered clearer.

7. Calvin, *Acts of the Council of Trent*, 3:152. For further use of the sun analogy, cf. *Institutes*, 3:11:6.

8. I [Chris] heard this example from Anthony N. S. Lane when he delivered Wheaton College's History of Christianity Lecture in 2012, a talk entitled "Justification by Works in Reformation Theology."

9. For example, according to Peter Martyr Vermigli, the notion that one can merit divine favor for oneself is completely unacceptable. He asserts, "Therefore, we must take away all merit, not only in those who are not yet justified, but also in those who have been justified." It is only by the merit of Christ (*solus Christi merito*) that one is justified. Vermigli, *Romanos*, 1289 [195]; 1321 [227]. Cf. Calvin, *Institutes*, 3:15.2.

10. With regard to rewards, the Westminster Confession of Faith asserts: "Notwithstanding, the persons of believers being accepted through Christ, their good works also are accepted in Him; not as though they were in this life wholly unblamable and unreproveable in God's sight but that He, looking upon them in His Son, is pleased to accept and reward that which is sincere, although accompanied with many weaknesses and imperfections" (16.6).

11. This is true in Catholic biblical studies and theology alike. Joseph A. Fitzmyer, for instance, argues in his exegesis of Romans 3:28 that "in this context Paul means [to teach justification] 'by faith alone.'" Fitzmyer also provides support for *sola fide* from patristic and medieval interpreters. Fitzmyer, *Romans* (New York: Doubleday, 1993), 360–363. In Pope

Benedict's sermon on justification (November 19, 2008), he affirmed, "Being just simply means being with Christ and in Christ. And this suffices. Further observances are no longer necessary. For this reason Luther's phrase: 'faith alone' is true, if it is not opposed to faith in charity in love." Pope Benedict XVI, *Saint Paul* (San Francisco: Ignatius, 2009), 82. A week later (November 26, 2008), the pontiff continued this emphasis: "Following Saint Paul, we have seen that man is unable to 'justify' himself with his own actions, but can only truly become 'just' before God because God confers his 'justice' upon him, uniting him to Christ his Son. And man obtains this union through faith. In this sense, Saint Paul tells us: not our deeds, but rather faith renders us 'just.'" Ibid., 84. Finally, according to the Annex to the Joint Declaration on the Doctrine of Justification, "Justification takes place 'by grace alone' . . . by faith alone; the person is justified 'apart from works'" (2.C). The Annex is accessible at: http://www.vatican.va/roman_curia/pontifical_councils/chrstuni/documents/rc_pc_chrstuni_doc_31101999_cath-luth-annex_en.html.

12. According to the Council of Trent, faith must be augmented by the infusion of charity by the Holy Spirit. "For faith, unless hope and charity be added to it, neither unites one perfectly with Christ, nor makes one a living member of his body." *Canons and Decrees of the Council of Trent*, 6th session (January 13, 1547), *Decree on Justification*, 8, in Schaff, 2:97.

13. *Canons and Decrees of the Council of Trent*, 6th session (January 13, 1547), *Decree on Justification*, chaps. 9, 13; canons 15, 16; in Schaff, 2:98–99; 103–104; 113–114. According to this last canon, one exception to this denial of assurance of salvation exists: one has learned this by special revelation.

14. Ibid., canon 22; in Schaff, 2:115.

15. Ibid., canon 23; in Schaff, 2:115.

16. *JD*, 34.

17. *JD*, 36.
18. Ibid.
19. The closing sentence of the Catholic position says, "Recognizing [the justified person's] own failures, however, the believer may yet be certain that God intends his salvation." Ibid.
20. The other two aspects of Christ's body are "the Church militant" (on earth) and "the Church triumphant" (in heaven).

Chapter 7: The Gospel of Jesus Christ: Hope for Both Protestants and Catholics

1. John Owen, *The Doctrine of Justification by Faith*, chap. VII, "Imputation, and the Nature of It," in *The Works of John Owen*, 16 vols. (Edinburgh: Banner of Truth, 1998), 5:163–164; quoted in John Piper, *The Future of Justification* (Wheaton, Ill.: Crossway, 2007), 25.
2. Philip Ryken, *My Father's World: Meditations on Christianity and Culture*. (Phillipsburg, N.J.: P&R, 2002), 230–231.
3. After all, the Catholic Church still anathematizes Protestant teaching with the canons of Trent (not every Protestant agrees with the details of the *JD*).
4. Leonardo De Chirico, *A Christian's Pocket Guide to the Papacy: Its Origins and Role in the 21ˢᵗ Century* (Scotland: Christian Focus, 2014). De Chirico discusses the history of this identification.
5. Martin Luther, *Lecture on Galatians 1535*, in *LW*, 26:24.
6. John Calvin and Jacopo Sadoleto, *A Reformation Debate: Sadoleto's Letter to the Genevans and Calvin's Reply*, ed. John C. Olin (New York: Harper Torchbooks, 1966), 69.
7. Charles Hodge's Letter to Pope Pius IX, 1869, reprinted in *Banner of Truth*, November 5, 2010, https://banneroftruth.org/us/resources/articles/2010/charles-hodges-letter-to-pope-pius-ix/. The text has been rendered clearer. Hodge wrote the letter on

behalf of the two General Assemblies of the Presbyterian Church in the United States.

8. Avery Cardinal Dulles, "Justification in Contemporary Theology," in *Justification by Faith: Lutherans and Catholics in Dialogue VII*, ed. H. George Anderson, et al. (Minneapolis, Minn.: Augsburg, 1985), 256. According to Lane, even if the *Joint Declaration on the Doctrine of Justification* is taken into account, the positive exposition of Trent's decree remains incompatible with a Protestant understanding, even though the gap is narrower than it was previously. Lane, *Justification by Faith*, 223.

9. Lane, *Justification by Faith*, 85.

10. Cyprian, *Letter* 72.21, in *ANF*, 5:384.

11. *Lumen Gentium*, 14–17.

12. *Canons and Decrees of the Council of Trent*, 6th session (January 13, 1547), *Decree on Justification*, 16, in Schaff, 2:108.

13. The citation is from Thérèse of Lisieux, "Act of Offering," in *Story of a Soul*, trans. John Clarke (Washington, D.C.: ICS, 1981), 27.

14. Dulles, "Justification in Contemporary Theology," 258.

15. Ibid.

16. Thérèse of Lisieux, "Act of Offering," 27.

Conclusion: Is the Reformation Finished?

1. Peter Kreeft, "Ecumenical Jihad," in *Reclaiming The Great Tradition*, ed. James S. Cutsinger (Downers Grove, Ill.: InterVarsity, 1997), 27.

2. T.S. Eliot, *Four Quartets*.

Historical Theology

An Introduction to Christian Doctrine

Gregg R. Allison

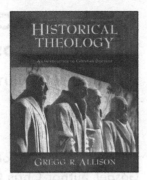

Most historical theology texts follow Christian beliefs chronologically, discussing notable doctrinal developments for all areas of theology according to their historical appearance. And while this may be good history, it can make for confusing theology, with the classic theological loci scattered throughout various time periods, movements, and controversies. In *Historical Theology*, Gregg Allison offers students the opportunity to study the historical development of theology according to a topical-chronological arrangement, setting out the history of Christian doctrine one theological element at a time. Such an approach allows readers to concentrate on one tenet of Christianity and its formulation in the early church, through the Middle Ages, Reformation, and post-Reformation era, and into the modern period. The text includes a generous mix of primary source material as well, citing the words of Cyprian, Augustine, Aquinas, Luther, Calvin, Barth, and others. Allison references the most accessible editions of these notable theologians' work so that readers can continue their study of historical theology through Christian history's most important contributors. *Historical Theology* is a superb resource for those familiar with Wayne Grudem's *Systematic Theology* or interested in understanding the development of Christian theology.

Talking with Catholics about the Gospel

A Guide for Evangelicals

Chris Castaldo

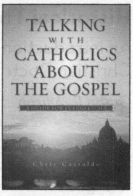

In *Talking with Catholics about the Gospel*, author Chris Castaldo provides an easy-to-follow introduction to basic Catholic belief and practice, equipping evangelical Protestants for more fruitful spiritual conversations. Written in accessible, non-technical language, this short book offers readers:

- A more informed awareness of Catholicism
- Encouragement to move from a combative posture to a gracious one
- Clarification of erroneous caricatures of Catholics in favor of a more constructive understanding

Based in part on Castaldo's experience as a Catholic and time spent working professionally in the Catholic Church, *Talking with Catholics about the Gospel* gives readers a framework for recognizing where lines of similarity and difference fall between Catholics and evangelical Protestants, along with handy tips for engaging in spiritual discussions.

Readers will gain encouragement and practical insights for gracious and worthwhile discussions of faith with Catholic believers.

Available in stores and online!

ZONDERVAN®
.com

Holy Ground

Walking with Jesus as a Former Catholic

Chris Castaldo

> *"This is the best book I have read that chronicles such pilgrimages. And it is full of godly commonsense."*
> —D. A. Carson, Research Professor of New Testament, Trinity Evangelical Divinity School

> *"A refreshing change...[Castaldo] shows respect for the tradition from which he departed"*
> —Francis J. Beckwith, Professor of Philosophy and Church-State Studies, Baylor University. Author of *Return to Rome: Confessions of an Evangelical Catholic.*

> *"Very important [and] very helpful!"*
> —J. I. Packer, Professor of Theology, Regent College

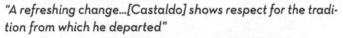

Do you dread conversation at Christmas dinner with your Catholic family? At weddings, funerals, and holidays? Chris Castaldo has wrestled personally with this question and many more. Perhaps you have too. Whether you are a former Roman Catholic or know someone who is, you'll find helpful answers and encouraging support within these pages. Like: how can Evangelicals and Catholics reach such different conclusions from the same Scripture? When I talk about my faith with my Catholic family, why does someone always get upset? How does my Catholic background still influence my views of God and salvation? And how should I talk with my Catholic friends about Jesus? More than providing historical perspective, theological reflection, and practical lessons, *Holy Ground* is a dynamic exploration of how to emulate both the grace and truth of the Lord Jesus Christ in relation to the Catholic people you love.